Key Tools of
WRITING & RESEARCH:
A Guide for the Student Writer

Kendall Hunt
publishing company

Cassandra L. Baker, PhD

Kendall Hunt
publishing company

www.kendallhunt.com
Send all inquiries to:
4050 Westmark Drive
Dubuque, IA 52004-1840

Copyright © 2020 by Kendall Hunt Publishing Company

ISBN: 978-1-7924-0099-5

Published in the United States of America

Dedication

To my father, Mr. Clarence Baker (1933–2018):
Thank you for blessing me with the gift of perseverance and exploration.
Thank you for your wisdom and support.
You were a true maverick.

To my mother, Mrs. Beatrice Baker:
Thank you for pushing me to publish over the last twenty years.
You are the ultimate mother.

Both of you believed in me before I believed in myself,
guided me when I could not guide myself.
Your love and devotion are unprecedented.

Epigraph

Write down the vision
and make it plain and clear on tablets
so that a herald may run with it.
For the vision awaits an appointed time;
it speaks of the end
and will not prove false.
Though it lingers, wait for it;
it will certainly come
and will not delay.

—Habakkuk 2:2–3
New International Version (NIV)

About the Author

Cassandra L. Baker, PhD, is an instructor of business management at Gwinnett Technical College. Dr. Baker previously worked in the school of business and school of humanities at the University of Phoenix teaching various business courses at the graduate and undergraduate levels, including writing and research. Prior to joining academia, Cassandra spent fifteen years with Ford Motor Company and Volvo Cars of North America. She is a highly accomplished executive with experience in franchise management, organization management, financial management, and strategic planning within marketing sales and service.

Cassandra has held various executive positions within Ford and Volvo, starting with dealer development and then moving on to business management, best practices and process development, ISO lead auditor, market representation, and network project management. Cassandra took her experience overseas, working in the United Kingdom, Sweden, and China. During her time in Europe, she worked with national sales companies and dealers in European Union Accession countries creating project plans to help dealers become profitable.

Cassandra holds a PhD in organization and management from Capella University, an MBA from Brenau University, and a BS in business administration from Shorter University. Her continuing education background includes professional training as a Six Sigma Black Belt and Green Belt, a Certified Sarbanes-Oxley professional, an ISO lead auditor, and a team leader Myers-Briggs certification. Dr. Baker founded Prama Publishing and Sugar Hill Research and Consulting on her belief in sharing knowledge and assisting students and organizations in achieving their goals to create win-win situations for all involved.

Contents

List of Figures

CHAPTER 5

CHAPTER 6

Preface

As a business instructor over the past eighteen years, all I have heard from students is "I am not a good writer." This phrase has come from traditional and non-traditional students. After reading numerous papers over the years, it occurred to me that today's students are unique because in almost every aspect of their lives there is a software application to assist in accomplishing tasks. In general, the current writing textbooks are good, but few discuss the tools of writing and how you use those tools to become a more proficient writer. *Key Tools of Writing and Research* fills the gap. This book does not focus on grammar and syntax; its focus is on the required tools needed from the beginning to the end of the writing process.

The Writing Process

Key Tools of Writing and Research gives the student writer a clear guide by combining Internet searches, library databases, structured analytical techniques, rhetorical modes, software applications, and checklists. Students will see the process of writing is easier once the necessary tools and techniques are put into practice. This textbook takes a quality-management view of writing. In quality management, the focus is on continuous improvement through the use of principles, practices, tools, and techniques.

The key tools contained within this book allow students to implement the following quality-management methods:

- Research and understand the needs of the student, instructor, and assignment.
- Establish a clear vision of the assignment.
- Set goals and targets for class.
- Provide students with required resources to write responsibly and establish accountability for individual and team assignments.
- Encourage students to recognize and understand the contributions of scholars.
- Accept and take ownership of writing problems.
- Embrace opportunities to enhance knowledge, experience, and skill in writing and research.
- Present clear responsibility for the writing process and accountability for managing key steps.
- Supply students with training in processes, procedures, and tools for continuous improvement in writing.
- Ensure that data and information are current, relevant, accurate, reliable, and valid.
- Create clear and open communication for team activities and sharing of information.

Chapter Overview

Chapter 1

Part of assessing an assignment is assessing your software resources. Chapter 1 is called "Getting Writing Ready" because it aids the student in programming their Word processor to comply with writing and style guidelines. I use Microsoft Word for the software application and *American Psychological Association* (APA) style to illustrate what it takes for compliance. Additionally, this chapter discusses Internet browsers and other software applications needed for effective research and writing.

The main objective in this chapter is to get students ready for writing. This means assessing the assignment and knowledge assets available through libraries and the Internet. Contingency planning is an important part of "getting writing ready" so the student will not panic in the face of an emergency. Most importantly, Chapter 1 allows the student to understand the necessary software applications needed to use a computer while in school. For example, Adobe DC opens PDF files; Adobe Flash plays videos. Moreover, students are first introduced to writing and style guidelines. The student learns how to use the settings in Microsoft Word to adhere to these guidelines on their computer.

Chapter 2

The first stage of the writing process is prewriting. This chapter covers the basic prewriting activities when writing an essay or research paper. Chapter 2 brings a fresh perspective to prewriting activities by creating synergy and combining rhetorical modes of writing, logical order, and structured analytical techniques used in process management.

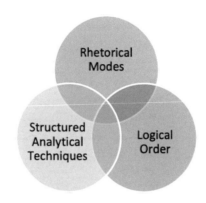

Rhetorical modes are how people communicate. Logical order creates principles of organization, and process management uses analytical tools to enhance students' ability to structure and organize their ideas. Each rhetorical mode is matched with an analytical quality tool that is used in process management. Students will be able to identify the right analytical tools to make the rhetorical mode.

Chapter 3

Outlining is the second stage in the writing process. Chapter 3 is exciting because the purpose of an outline is discussed as a strategy that has a distinct pattern, position, perspective, and ploy that assist in making every writing assignment unique. Within Chapter 3, instructions are given on how to create an outline, how the outline integrates into the writing process, team management, time management, and logical order. Finally, students are shown how outlining is used in Microsoft Word and how it integrates with Microsoft PowerPoint.

Chapter 4

Research and analysis are at the heart of academic writing. Chapter 4 discusses how to begin writing a paper using annotated outlines and annotated bibliographies. It introduces a modified annotated outline-bibliography. Finally, it covers the software applications used for annotation.

Chapter 5

The Internet and Wikipedia are students' first choices for acquiring supporting information used for research projects. Chapter 5 teaches Internet research using Google Special Syntax and Bing Query Language. Students learn how to use Wikipedia proactively without citing it as an actual source. They also learn about following the bibliographic trail and temporal citations to assist in locating viable research sources.

Chapter 6

Chapter 6 begins teaching students how to evaluate information and the validity of peer-reviewed articles. Next, it distinguishes between discovery and federated searching when using the major aggregators. Chapter 6 discusses these aggregators, portals, and open-source discovery tools, including EBSCO, ProQuest, Google Scholar, and Directory of Open Access Journals (DOAJ). It also includes other sources such as Microsoft Academic and the ACI Scholarly Blog Index. Chapter 6 allows the student to gain a clear understanding of the research sources available through their college or university library.

Chapter 7

After completing the research, one of the biggest questions is "How do I keep track of all of this stuff?" Chapter 7 answers this question in discussing the importance of using a reference or bibliographic manager as a personal research assistant to house all the research collected. By using reference-bibliographic managers, students will learn that they are creating a personal database of information for each paper they write. We will review the major reference managers Zotero, Mendeley, RefWorks, and EndNote.

Chapter 8

Revising and editing is another stage in the writing process. Chapter 8 discusses these stages and provides checklists as tools for editing and proofreading. Students learn that they must follow REAP (revising, editing, accuracy, proofreading) to create a good paper. Software tools for editing and proofreading are reviewed.

Chapter 9

Chapter 9 is important because it examines plagiarism. The meaning, types, causes, punishment, and prevention of plagiarism are talked about in detail. Most importantly, students' responsibility for originality is outlined and detailed along with software tools to prevent plagiarism.

Chapter 10

Bringing all the components together is the topic of discussion for Chapter 10. Chapter 10 talks about paragraph development, grade rubrics, and transition words. Step-by-step instructions are given on constructing a paper from a topic or given instructions.

Teaching the Text

This book is designed to be used as a stand-alone text or a companion guide to further develop the writing process. Each chapter contains end-of-chapter material including review questions, definitions, and keywords that will assist the student in understanding main concepts. The review questions are based on Bloom's taxonomy, allowing the student to develop various levels of critical thinking. The keywords will extend the student's technical vocabulary.

Companion Website

The website for this book contains summaries of key points, terminology for each chapter, templates, checklists, and links to the websites mentioned within the text. PowerPoints for teaching purposes will also be available. To get free access to these materials, go to www.keytoolsofwriting.com.

Acknowledgment

To William H. Heitjan,

Thank you for reviewing and giving constructive feedback during the creation of this book. Your love, loyalty, friendship, dedication, and support have helped me achieve this remarkable dream.

CHAPTER 1

Getting Writing Ready

Chapter Learning Objectives:

- Define and list student academic assets.
- Explain assessing the assignment.
- Discuss contingency planning.
- Discuss using a smartphone as an internet device.
- Understand author's responsibility and how it applies to the student writer.
- Identify and discuss the different writing and style guidelines.
- Demonstrate an understanding of the importance of formatting.
- Identify different internet browsers and why they are necessary.
- Identify additional software applications and extensions for improved multimedia interaction.

Assessing the Assignment

Assessing the assignment means understanding what the instructor is requesting. Students have an opportunity to ask clarifying questions and obtain guidance before the writing process begins. Asking the right questions could mean the difference between a good grade or a bad one. Think of assessing the assignment as a learning opportunity to grow as a scholar. The list below is a series of clarifying questions that should be answered before beginning an essay or research paper. Obtaining the answer to these questions will assist in guiding your writing project.

- What is the page length or word count of the assignment?
- Who is the audience?
- What are the objectives?
- Is this a team or individual assignment?
- Should the assignment be written following the *American Psychological Association* (APA), *Modern Language Association* (MLA), or *Chicago Manual of Style* (Chicago) guidelines?
- What is the due date?

- How should the assignment be submitted?
- Does the instructor want a plagiarism report? What is the allowed similarity index? Five or 10 percent?
- Should the assignment be written in the first person or the third person?
- Is this an essay or research paper?
- Did the instructor give a list of topics or questions/statements to answer? If it is a topic, then identify key concepts and deliverables.
- Did the instructor create an outline for the assignment? An outline can be a great help during the prewriting process.
- What is the minimum number of required scholarly references?
- Is an abstract required?
- Is an annotated outline or annotated bibliography required?
- Is a grade rubric available?

STUDENT KNOWLEDGE ASSETS

Another crucial step in assessing the assignment is taking inventory of your knowledge assets and knowledge management. "Knowledge management involves the process of identifying, capturing, organizing, and using knowledge assets to create and sustain competitive advantage" (Evans & Lindsay, 2016, p. 620). **Knowledge assets** are the tools and resources available to a student to assist in the writing process. Academic assets include:

knowledge assets

The tools and resources available to a student to assist in the writing process.

- Lecture notes
- Textbooks
- Software applications
- Writing and style guides
- Libraries—Journals, books, articles, magazines, databases
- Dictionaries
- Thesauruses
- Writing Centers
- Calendar systems (such as Google Calendar)
- Plagiarism checkers
- Reference managers
- File storage plans (Google Drive, Microsoft OneDrive, flash drives)

CONTINGENCY PLAN

contingency plan

A backup plan created for emergencies.

Finally, think about a contingency plan. A **contingency plan** is a backup plan of what you would do if your computer fails, the Internet is down, the power goes out, or servers go down. Below are suggestions for creating a solid contingency plan:

- Write down the types of problems that may occur or that have happened in the past.
- Talk with your instructor about alternative ways to submit assignments in case of an emergency.

- Use your smartphone as an alternative. Check your data plan, because your smartphone is a mini computer and can be used as a **mobile hotspot**, which can connect to your main computer to search the Internet and submit assignments.
- Download the mobile app for your college or university learning-management system. The major learning-management systems Blackboard, D2L, and Moodle all have mobile applications that can be downloaded from Google Play, Microsoft Store, or Apple Store.
- Locate nearby establishments that provide free Wi-Fi. These could include grocery stores, coffee houses, cafes, or libraries. In Google Play or Apple Store, there is a free application called WiFi Map (www.wifimap.io) that will find all of the location establishments based on your location with free Wi-Fi.
- Use some form of cloud technology such as Google Drive or Microsoft OneDrive as a backup to save your work.

mobile hotspot

Travel routers that allow internet access from a smartphone.

Microsoft Word Readiness

Many students are often confused on how to begin a writing assignment. Usually, the student begins researching the writing assignment on the Internet without the knowledge of preparation, search strategies, or structure. Students are unaware that writing is a beautiful process that can be trusted and used repeatedly.

Before you begin writing, it is essential that your **word processor** is set up for writing. When you buy word-processing software, the settings are standard factory settings. Factory settings do not comply with the writing style, rules, and guidelines adopted by your college.

word processor

Software application that is used for writing, printing, and publishing of the written word.

Writing styles are "a simple set of procedures that codify the many components of scientific writing to increase the ease of reading comprehension" (American Psychological Association [APA], 2010, xiii). Some colleges use different writing styles depending on the college and course major. There are many writing styles, including Harvard, Turabian, and Chicago. The three most adopted styles are APA, MLA, and Chicago.

American Psychological Association (APA)

Writing and style guidelines used in studies of the behavioral and social sciences.

APA is used in studies of the behavioral and social sciences (APA, 2006). These include disciplines or college majors such as business, information technology, psychology, sociology, economics, criminology, education, and nursing.

Modern Language Association (MLA)

Modern Language Association writing and style guidelines, often found in the schools of humanities and liberal arts.

MLA is often found in the schools of humanities and liberal arts. Disciplines include comparative literary analysis, cultural studies, English studies in language and literature, foreign language and literature, and literary criticism.

Chicago Style is used in the publishing industry. If you were writing to publish a book, then this is what you would use. Whether your style is Chicago, MLA, or APA, you must first get writing ready. For the purpose of this book, the APA manual, sixth edition will be used.

Chicago Manual of Style (Chicago)

Writing and style guidelines widely used in the publishing industry.

author's responsibility

Accuracy and integrity of a written paper, including formatting according to writing and style guidelines.

What does it mean to get writing ready? In the twenty-first century, word processors are now the writing vehicle of choice. Writers must ensure that their word processor is ready to handle their chosen style. The APA refers to this as "author's responsibility." The author's responsibility includes typeface (font size), line spacing, margins, paragraphs and indentations, page numbers, and spelling and grammar checking. A word processor can assist the writer in meeting these responsibilities. Additionally, it is the responsibility of the author/student/researcher to submit well-prepared papers to instructors. A well-prepared paper allows the reader to correctly interpret content. When an instructor sees a well-prepared paper that is formatted correctly and free of spelling errors, then feedback is centered on content and correcting errors in logic.

Microsoft Word

Word-processing software application.

Word processors assist the writer in implementing the writing process more quickly and efficiently by authoring, formatting, and publishing your work (Lambert & Cox, 2013)—basically, ensuring that the Microsoft Word formatting is APA, MLA, or Chicago compliant. Formatting refers to the layout of the paper, which is an important first step in ensuring academic success.

formatting

Refers to the layout of the paper.

Formatting Font

font

Typeface.

Using a uniform font enhances readability, reduces eye fatigue, and improves the visual presentation of the paper (APA, 2010). Too many different fonts in a document cause it to appear as a ransom note or plagiarizing rather than an academic paper. Ensure that your font is consistent throughout. The figures in this chapter were created using Microsoft Word 2016. Note that Office 365, Word 2013, and 2010 have basically the same steps for formatting. Below are the APA guidelines to begin correctly formatting a paper:

- Use 12-point Times New Roman, Arial, or Courier font in your academic papers.
- To set the font and style, select the Home tab. From the Font toolbar, you may adjust the font, size, and style to the correct format.
- Use italics (sparingly) for emphasis instead of bold, underlining, or all capital letters.
- Eliminate bold text, except for use with paragraph headings (Figure 1.1).

FIGURE 1.1

Formatting Font

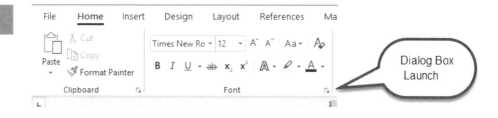

KEY TOOLS OF WRITING AND RESEARCH *A Guide for the Student Writer*

To set a **default** font:

1. Click the **dialog box launcher**.
2. Click either Times New Roman, Arial, or Courier.
3. Set font as 12-point font.
4. Click **Set As Default**.
5. Select **All documents based on the Normal template** (Figure 1.2).

default

Options that are preselected by a computer software application.

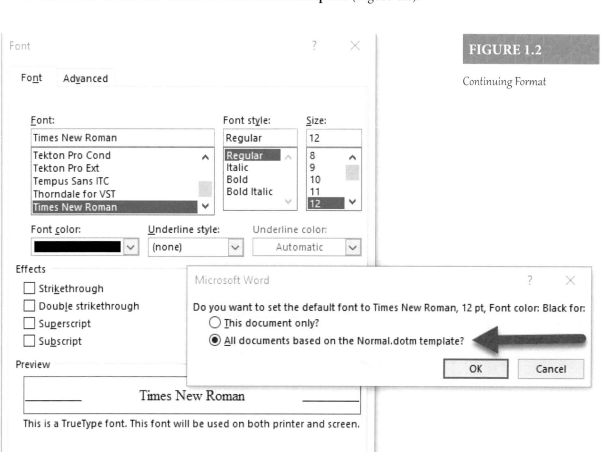

FIGURE 1.2

Continuing Format

Now, every time you open your Microsoft Word document, it will open with the same chosen font.

Formatting Margins

Margins should be uniform. Use 1-inch (2.54 cm) margins throughout the paper (top, bottom, sides). Uniform margins augment readability and provide a dependable measure for estimating the length of a paper (APA, 2010; McGuire, Gerber, & Currin, 2001).

The directions below demonstrate how to set your margins properly in Word:

1. Select the **Layout** tab.
2. In the Layout menu, the **Margins** button will allow you to change the margins to the correct format (Figure 1.3).

FIGURE 1.3

Formatting Margins

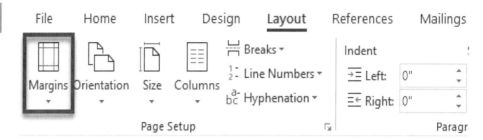

3. Choose any of the other options in the Margins gallery to change margins; each one shows the margin measurements.

4. If you want the new margins to be the default every time you open Microsoft Word, choose **Margins**, then **Custom Margins**. In the Page Setup dialog box, on the Margins tab, choose **Set As Default**, then **Yes**, then **OK** (Figure 1.4).

FIGURE 1.4

Formatting Custom Margins

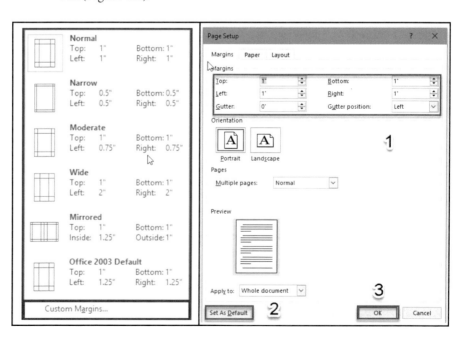

KEY TOOLS OF WRITING AND RESEARCH *A Guide for the Student Writer*

Formatting Line Spacing

The body of your paper should contain double spacing. Also double-space after every line in your title, heading, indented quotations, and references.

1. Select the text you want to change.
2. On the **Home** tab, click **Line and Paragraph Spacing**.
3. Click on **2.0** for double spacing (Figure 1.5).

Paragraphs and Indentation

The first line of every paragraph must be indented five to seven spaces, or half an inch. Once you indent the first paragraph, continue to type the remaining lines of the paper using left-hand margins. Use the Tab key on your keyboard to indent half an inch. If you want to make exact changes to your indents in Microsoft Word, follow these steps:

1. Select one paragraph or a group of paragraphs that you want to adjust.
2. Click the **Paragraph dialog box launcher** on the Page Layout or Layout tab (Figure 1.6).

3. If necessary, choose the **Indents and Spacing** tab.
4. Choose your settings, and then choose **OK** (Figure 1.7).

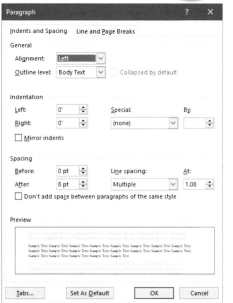

FIGURE 1.5

Formatting Line Spacing

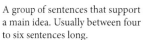

FIGURE 1.6

Paragraphs and Indentations

FIGURE 1.7

Paragraphs, Indentations, and Spacing

paragraph

A group of sentences that support a main idea. Usually between four to six sentences long.

indentation

One tab or five spaces in the word processor. A signal that a new paragraph is beginning.

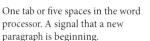

ruler

Used in most word-processing programs; it measures the layout on a page.

Ruler

The easier method is to use the **ruler** feature in Microsoft Word. Within MS Word, the ruler assists in aligning text, graphs, and tables. Activating the ruler is extremely helpful for aligning your reference page (Figures 1.8 and 1.9).

FIGURE 1.8

Ruler

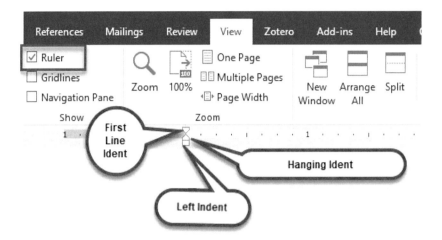

FIGURE 1.9

Ruler-Indentation Explanation

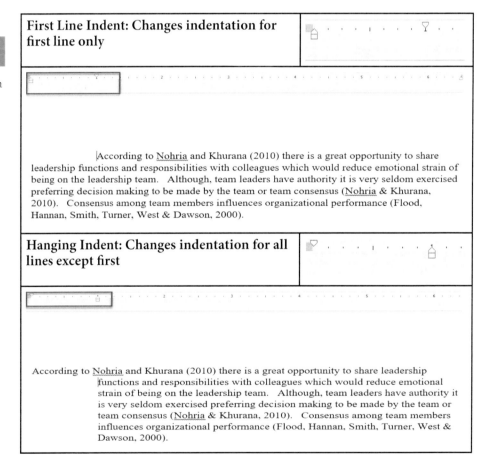

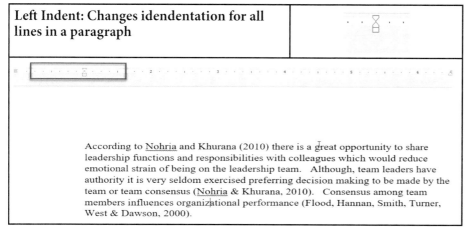

| Left Indent: Changes idendentation for all lines in a paragraph |  |

> According to Nohria and Khurana (2010) there is a great opportunity to share leadership functions and responsibilities with colleagues which would reduce emotional strain of being on the leadership team. Although, team leaders have authority it is very seldom exercised preferring decision making to be made by the team or team consensus (Nohria & Khurana, 2010). Consensus among team members influences organizational performance (Flood, Hannan, Smith, Turner, West & Dawson, 2000).

page numbers

Number assigned to a document such as an essay or research paper. Locators to help find information in a book, journal, or article.

FIGURE 1.10

Insert Page Number

Formatting Page Number

Page number can be implemented before or after your paper is completed. The page header contains the page number aligned with the right margin. Microsoft Word should be used to insert consecutive **page numbers** within the paper. Arabic numerals (1, 2, 3) are used to number each page, starting with the title page. Automatic pagination allows the numbering of your document to flow from one page to another without having manually to number each one.

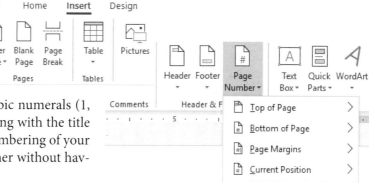

1. Choose **Insert**, then **Page Number**.
2. Choose **Top of Page**.
3. Choose **Plain Number 3** in the Style Gallery (Figures 1.10 and 1.10.1).

Headings

Headings are an essential part of organization within your paper. APA has five levels of headings, and each level establishes a hierarchy of sections within a paper to create format and appearance. Headings are important

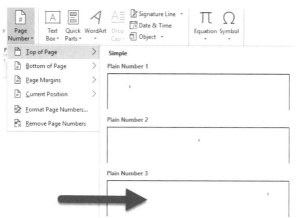

FIGURE 1.10.1

Insert Page Number, Con.

heading

The title at the beginning of a page, new paragraph, or book chapter.

heading levels

Formatting arrangements of headings.

in organizing ideas, which allows a paper to have effective flow. Programming **heading levels** is essential in Microsoft Word because they connect with several other funtionalities, such as the Table of Contents (McGuire et al., 2001). More will be discussed about headings in later chapters.

FIGURE 1.11

Heading Levels

FORMAT FOR FIVE LEVELS OF HEADINGS	
Level of Information	**Text Example**
Level 1	**Heading 1** Centered and Boldface in Upper and Lowercase Heading
Level 2	**Heading 2** Flush Left, Boldface in Uppercase and Lowercase Heading
Level 3	**Heading 3.** Indented, boldface, lowercase paragraph heading ending with a period
Level 4	***Heading 4.*** Indented, boldface, italicized, lowercase paragraph heading ending with a period
Level 5	*Heading 5.* Indented, italicized, lowercase paragraph ending with a period

Use heading levels to create organization in your work if your paper is over three or four pages. Do not use them for short documents; it will make the paper appear rough. Ask your instructor if they are required for the assignment (Figure 1.11).

To format your heading levels in Microsoft Word, follow these steps:

FIGURE 1.12

Style Gallery

1. Select **Home**.
2. Right-click on **Heading 1** in the Style Gallery, then select **Modify** (Figure 1.12).
3. Name heading level.

Styles

FIGURE 1.13

Style Gallery Modification

4.   Modify all items according to Figure 1.13

After all items are selected, then click **OK**. It would be feasible to modify five

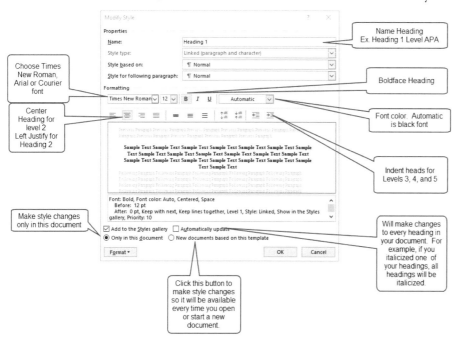

FIGURE 1.14

Modify Style Explanation

different levels of headings. After modifying Heading 1, Heading 2 should automatically become available. Modify Heading 2 according to the APA in Figure 1.14. Remember, modify all five heading levels based on the requirements of the APA format.

Spelling and Grammar Checking

Checking your grammar and spelling is critical to readability and validity in writing. Often, many students will write a paper neglecting to check their spelling and grammar. When an instructor reviews your paper and notices numerous and obvious spelling and grammar issues, it sets the tone for how they will grade your work. "Uncorrected grammatical errors, misspelled words, and typographical mistakes can all distract from the effectiveness of your paper" (Rampolla, 2015, p. 72). Style and grammar errors can obscure the purpose of your paper and make it difficult to read and follow. A well-constructed essay or research paper uses correct grammar, punctuation, and spelling (Vojak, Kline, Cope, McCarthey, & Kalantzis, 2011). Correct spelling, grammar, and punctuation allow for clear communication. Most word processors have adequate spelling, grammar, and style checkers. However, please note that this program does not take the place of proofreading. Microsoft Word performs sufficiently as a first-round proofreading tool. Follow these steps for modifying your Microsoft Word program to detect spelling, grammar, and style errors:

1. Click the **File** tab, and then click **Options**.
2. Click **Proofing**.
3. Under **When correcting spelling and grammar in Word**, click **Settings**.
4. Click all options under **Grammar**.
5. Once all options are selected, then click **OK** (Figure 1.15).

FIGURE 1.15

Proofing

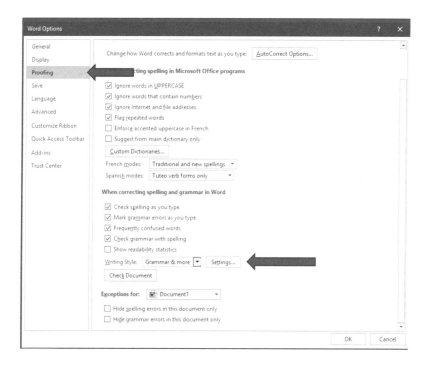

KEY TOOLS OF WRITING AND RESEARCH *A Guide for the Student Writer*

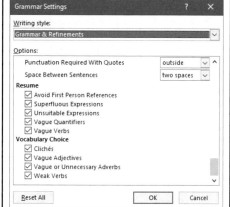

FIGURE 1.16

Grammar and Settings

In Microsoft Word 2016, the writing style menu has two options: "Grammar" or "Grammar & more." Either option can be chosen, but it is best when writing academic papers to choose "Grammar & more" to gain the most value out of the spelling and grammar feature (Microsoft, 2017). Once the grammar setting has been programmed in Microsoft Word, it is now equipped to assist in editing (Figure 1.16).

Internet Browsers

An **internet browser** is a software program that allows access to the Internet and viewing web content on the computer. More than one browser should be installed on your computer. Having more than one is not only practical; it is critical. The biggest concern is browser compatibility. Web and cloud-based applications may have a preferred browser for optimum usability.

internet browser

Software program that allows access to the internet to view web content on the computer.

Additionally, learning-management systems such as Blackboard may operate better with Firefox or Chrome and not Microsoft Edge, which is the former Internet Explorer. As of January 2016, Microsoft no longer supports older versions of the Internet Explorer. The only version of the Internet Explorer that will be supported is Internet Explorer 11 (www.microsoft.com/en-us/windowsforbusiness/end-of-ie-support). Finally, instructors will have students download or read material from a textbook publisher's website. Often publishers' web content may have a preferred browser.

All of the above-mentioned Internet browsers support plug-ins, extensions, and add-ons, which are helper programs to customize the browsing experience. Plug-ins assist better in searching, language support, news, and much more. Not every browser has the same add-ons or plug-ins. For example, Google Chrome has an add-on for mind mapping, whereas Firefox, MS Edge, and Opera do not. Different browsers are needed to support the writing process (Figure 1.17).

FIGURE 1.17

Internet Browsers

Internet browser name	Where to download	Company website
tanuha2001/Shutterstock.com	www.mozilla.org/en-US/firefox/new/?scene=2	www.mozilla.org/en-US/firefox/products
rvlsoft/Shutterstock.com	www.google.com/chrome	www.google.com
Microsoft Edge — rafapress/Shutterstock.com	www.microsoft.com/en-us/download/details.aspx?id=48126	www.microsoft.com
Denys Prykhodov/Shutterstock.com	support.apple.com/downloads/safari	www.apple.com
Rose Carson/Shutterstock.com	www.opera.com	www.opera.com/about

Keep all Internet browsers updated with the latest versions to ensure security and reliability. Update My Browser (updatemybrowser.org) is a good web-based tool that checks each browser for the latest version. Open each browser and go to updatemybrowser.org, and then the open-source website will check your browser for the latest version.

Additional Necessary Software

ADOBE READER

Adobe Reader allows you to interact with a Portable Document Format (PDF). Your computer can download PDF files without Adobe Reader. However, these files open in your Internet browser, which makes it difficult to interact with the PDF. Interacting with a PDF includes viewing, printing, signing, and annotating PDFs. The current version is Adobe DC, which can be downloaded from the Adobe DC Reader site (get.adobe.com/reader).

ADOBE FLASH PLAYER

Adobe Flash allows the user to play multimedia content such as audio, images, animations, and videos. If you cannot play a YouTube video, then it could be because you do not have a Flash plug-in (get.adobe.com/flashplayer).

JAVA

Java is a plug-in that works inside an Internet browser. Many websites and multimedia use Java to assist in running applications (apps). Java technology allows the user to play online games, chat with other people, use instant messaging, or view 3D images. Your computer does not need Java to operate efficiently. However, your Internet browser may need it to view certain websites. If so, then the website will notify you when you enter the site or perform an action that requires Java. To download Java, go to www.java.com/en.

MICROSOFT OFFICE COMPATIBILITY PACK

Students using a version of Word earlier than 2003 can install the free Microsoft Office Compatibility Pack for Word, Excel, and PowerPoint file formats from the Microsoft Download Center at www.microsoft.com/en-us/download. The Compatibility Pack enables older versions of Word to open the newer.docx files. A.docx file cannot be opened in Word 2003 or an earlier version of Word unless the person using that version installs the Microsoft Office Compatibility Pack.

Summary

Get ready, get set, and go! The main objective in Chapter 1 was to introduce the strategy of writing readiness. The message of this chapter is preparedness. Asking the right questions and developing a contingency plan gives students a tactical advantage in the writing process. Having the right Internet browsers and the additional software installed which are necessary to make the task of writing easier causes less stress. Students learn how to use Microsoft Word settings to become compliant with writing and style guidelines, such as the APA style.

Key Terms

American Psychological Association (APA)
Author's responsibility
Default
Font
Formatting
Heading
Heading levels
Indentation
Internet browser
Margins
Microsoft Word
Modern Language Association (MLA)
Page numbers
Paragraph
Ruler
Chicago Manual of Style (Chicago)
Word processor
Knowledge assets
Contingency plan
Mobile hotspot

Review Questions

1. Summarize the sixteen points of assessing an assignment.
2. Describe student knowledge assets and identify at least 10 assets in your college library.
3. Write a contingency plan for your essay or research paper.
4. List the resources needed for your contingency plan.
5. Identify when to use APA, MLA, or Chicago style.
6. Discuss the importance of formatting within a document.
7. Identify software applications that are needed on a computer before beginning to write.
8. Discuss how and why your Internet browser should be kept updated.
9. Identify the tools in this chapter to assist in writing.
10. Discuss why spelling and grammar are important in an essay or research paper.

References

American Psychological Association. (2010). *Publication Manual of the American Psychological Association,* (6th ed.). Washington, DC: American Psychological Association.

Evans, J. R., & Lindsay, W. M. (2016). *Managing for Quality and Performance Excellence* (10th ed.). Mason, OH: Cengage Learning.

Lambert, J., & Cox, J. (2013). *Microsoft Word 2013 Step By Step* (1st ed.). Redmond, WA: Microsoft Press.

McGuire, S. L., Gerber, D. E., & Currin, M. D. (2001). Helping students use APA format. *Journal of Nursing Education, 40*(9), 414–416. Retrieved from https://doi.org/10.3928/0148-4834-20011201-07.

Microsoft Corporation. (2017). Select grammar and writing style options in Word 2016–Support. Retrieved from https://support.office.com/en-us/article/Select-grammar-and-writing-style-options-in-Office-2016-ecd60e9f-6b2e-4070-b30c-42efa6cff55a?NS=WINWORD&Version=16&SysLcid=1033&UiLcid=1033&AppVer=ZWD160&HelpId=482&ui=en-US&rs=en-US&ad=US

Rampolla, M. L. (2015). *A pocket guide to writing in history* (8th ed.). Boston, MA: Bedford/St. Martin's.

Vojak, C., Kline, S., Cope, B., McCarthey, S., & Kalantzis, M. (2011). New spaces and old places: An analysis of writing assessment software. *Computers and Composition, 28*(2), 97–111. Retrieved from https://doi.org/10.1016/j.compcom.2011.04.004.

CHAPTER 2

Prewriting Strategies

Chapter Learning Objectives:

- Identify rhetorical mode classifications in writing.
- Identify the role of process management in prewriting strategies.
- Explain process-management tools matching rhetorical mode.
- Identify and discuss prewriting strategies.
- Explain the difference between convergent and divergent thinking.

Begin Prewriting with Research

Think of a process that occurs in everyday life: Driving to work. Making a morning cup of coffee. Performing tasks at a job. Writing is no different. Writing is a process; it has steps to achieve a goal, just like any other process. The steps in the writing process are:

1. Prewriting
2. Outlining
3. Drafting
4. Revising
5. Editing
6. Final Paper and Presentation

"**Prewriting** is the stage of the writing process during which you transfer your abstract thoughts into more concrete ideas in ink on paper" (McLean, 2011, p. 227). It is a critical step in the writing process. When you begin prewriting, you are in the stage of discovery. Discovery includes investigating your research topic and uncovering gaps in knowledge. The prewriting stage is also called invention because you are brainstorming and creating new ideas. **Research** is important at every stage of the writing process, but during the prewriting stage, knowing how to research is just as important as writing itself. The research will give you the words and evidence to effectively write and support your topic.

prewriting

The beginning stage of writing where the writer investigates a topic and writes their thoughts using paper or a computer.

research

Locating scholarly articles, journals, magazines, and websites as evidence to support a topic.

At almost every stage of the writing process, more research is required to refine your work. For example, if your paper does not meet the word count, that means more research. If your paper does not fully explain your topic, then more research is required. The prewriting stage offers a unique opportunity of discovery and enlightenment through the investigation of a topic. Take full advantage of the gift the prewriting stage offers.

FIGURE 2.1

Begin with Research

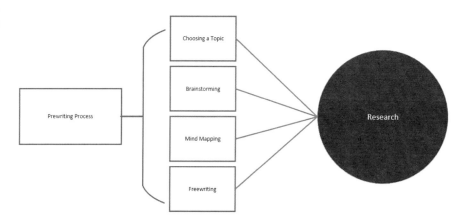

Before the writing process can begin, it must begin with scholarly research. Scholarly research is the foundation of a writing assignment. Research will allow brainstorming, mind mapping, and other idea-generation activities to take place. Within the writing process, students will dip into the research well many times before completing the final paper (Figure 2.1). Often, many students will say, "I am not a good writer." What the student is really saying is, "I am not a good reader, researcher, or both."

Students can be afraid of research. Do not be afraid. Other names for research are investigation, examination, and exploration of literature. Research gives students the words to write via summarizing, paraphrasing, or quoting. Without researching the past and current literature, students are writing based on their own limited knowledge. Explore aggregators such as EBSCO, ProQuest, or Gale to find scholarly peer-reviewed articles that provide evidentiary support for your paper. Research is collecting, reviewing, and analyzing information about your topic. Badke (2011) stated research should be used as a tool to:

1. Find the basics about a topic
2. Identify issues related to the topic
3. Analyze the topic
4. Potentially solve a problem or issue

Research is the foundation of a good paper.

Choosing a Topic

A **topic** is a broad subject that is usually a single word or a phrase. For example, gun control, universal healthcare, social media, and drugs are all topics. Students usually choose topics based on personal interest or professional significance. When choosing a topic, perform the following steps:

topic

A subject of discussion.

1. Research literature on the topic.
2. Ensure the topic is appropriate for the assignment.
3. Identify the rhetorical mode.
4. Confirm the topic is easily researchable.
5. Consider your audience.

When an instructor assigns a topic, it is usually easy to research, and the instructor wants you to learn an important concept. Most papers are an activity for learning, not reinventing the wheel or trying to solve world issues. JSTOR Labs has an application called Topicgraph (labs.jstor.org/topicgraph) that assists the student researcher in finding scholarly books from JSTOR's open-source book collection. According to JSTOR, "It helps researchers explore scholarly books by letting them understand at a glance all the topics covered within a book and then navigate directly to those pages about topics they're researching" (JSTOR Labs, 2017).

Brainstorming

Idea generation is an important stage in the writing process and is widely used as a creative and innovative activity. Alex Osborn (1957) pioneered brainstorming to improve the generation of ideas. Osborn (1957) had a set of four rules that individuals and groups must adhere to:

1. Generate as many ideas as possible. The more ideas, the better.
2. Do not criticize any idea. All ideas are worthy of consideration.
3. Attempt to combine any previously generated ideas.
4. Encourage wild and outrageous ideas, also called "freewheeling."

Brainstorming is an idea-generation activity allowing students to generate topics based on facts, impressions, emotions, and reactions (Litchfield, 2008; McWhorter, 2016). Brainstorming is an analytical activity that allows the student to find and identify relevant, variable, or driving forces of a topic (Heuer & Pherson, 2011). Depending on the type of paper the student is required to write, choosing the right brainstorming tool becomes more important.

brainstorming

An idea-generation activity that allows students to generate topic ideas based on facts, impressions, emotions, and reactions.

INDIVIDUAL BRAINSTORMING

Individual brainstorming is most effective for solving simple problems. Below are steps to individual brainstorming:

1. Choose a comfortable setting to think and create.
2. Think about your topic.
3. Set a time limit.
4. Write and record words.
5. Use stimuli to spark ideas, such as the Internet, word association, or brainstorming software.

TEAM OR GROUP BRAINSTORMING

Brainstorming also works in team settings. Group or team idea generation is called "structured brainstorming." Group brainstorming must be structured when involving more than one person because there are guidelines that must be followed. Creativity is enhanced by bouncing ideas off other people and generating a greater quantity of ideas than one person could generate alone (Heuer & Pherson, 2011). The twelve-step structured group brainstorming process was developed by the Central Intelligence Agency's Sherman Kent School for Intelligence Analysis (2009). The process is divided into two phases. The divergent-thinking phase involves the creative-thinking process: the generating and presenting of ideas. The convergent-thinking phase is the grouping, evaluation, and acceptance of ideas for use in a project.

divergent thinking

The creative thinking process; the generating and presenting of ideas.

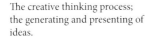

convergent thinking

The grouping, evaluation, and acceptance of ideas for use in a project.

Divergent-thinking phase:

1. Distribute sticky notes and pens or markers to all participants.
2. Pose the problem in terms of a focal question. Display it in one sentence on a large easel or whiteboard.
3. Ask the group to write down responses to the question, using keywords that will fit on the small sticky note.
4. Stick the notes on a wall for all to see. Treat every idea the same.
5. When a pause follows the initial flow of ideas, the group reaches the end of their conventional thinking, and new ideas are then likely to emerge.
6. Give participants a chance to say, "Pass, I do not have any ideas."
7. Keep brainstorming until everyone in the group says "pass."
8. End the idea-collection stage of the brainstorming after everyone has said "pass" at least twice. This lets the group leader know that all ideas have been exhausted.

Convergent-thinking phase:

1. Ask the group to rearrange the notes on the wall according to their commonalities or similar concepts. No talking is permitted. Some notes may be moved several times as notes begin to cluster. Copying notes is permitted so ideas can be included in more than one group, if necessary.
2. Select a word or phrase that characterizes each grouping or cluster once all the notes have been arranged.

3. Identify any notes that do not easily fit with others and consider them either useless noise or the beginning of an idea that deserves further attention.
4. Assess what the group has accomplished in terms of new ideas, concepts identified, or areas that need more work or further brainstorming.
5. Instruct each participant to select one or two areas that deserve the most attention. Tabulate the votes.
6. Set the group's priorities based on the voting and decide on the next steps for analysis.

Mind Mapping

Think of your paper as a product and your instructor as the customer. To enhance customer satisfaction, improve quality and value, and to create a vision for your product, mind maps are extremely helpful.

WHAT IS A MIND MAP?

Mind maps are visual representations of thoughts that create associations of ideas, which are connected by words, images, and how people think about a topic. It is a thinking tool, an outline, or a framework for the variables or subtopics, and it enhances creativity, group collaboration, problem-solving, study techniques, and memory retention. Mind maps are useful because they allow a large amount of information to be viewed at a glance (Budd, 2004; Davies, 2011; Dickinson, 2016; Dutt, 2015; Farrand, Hussain, & Hennessy, 2002; Heuer & Pherson, 2011; McWhorter, 2016; Tucker, Armstrong, & Massad, 2010).

mind maps

Visual representations of thoughts that create associations of ideas, which are connected by words, images, and how people think about a topic.

ADVANTAGES AND DISADVANTAGES OF MIND MAPPING

Chan (2004) discovered that mind mapping is a useful prewriting strategy that improves the skill and quality of students' writing. Ideas are free; there are no limits on ideas, which are free-form and flowing. Mind maps promote creativity and creative thinking. They encourage brainstorming and improve study techniques. Mind mapping is useful when taking class or meeting notes because one can be drawn quickly. In addition, it can improve memory recall because it allows for meaningful word association, knowledge links, and critical thinking. Mind maps capture the uniqueness of a writing assignment by accessing the writer's cognitive creativity and allow for a presentation of ideas. Finally, mind mapping enhances group collaboration (Davies, 2011; Dutt, 2015).

Although mind maps have many advantages and should be used by students, there are some disadvantages. Knowledge links are simple associations; there can be an absence of clear and direct links between topics. Furthermore, mind maps may be hard for others to read without some form of explanation. One of the biggest disadvantages is that mind maps are difficult to use for complex relationships. For example, mind mapping is not a great tool for relationship analysis; it is meant to explore the association between concepts (Davies, 2011; Tucker, Armstrong, & Massad, 2010).

HOW TO MAKE AND READ A MIND MAP

Pioneer Toney Buzan (2002) in his groundbreaking work on mind mapping developed a process called the seven laws of mind mapping. Buzan and Buzan (1996) stated:

1. Start with a blank page in a landscape (horizontal) layout. According to Buzan and Buzan (1996), this allows the brain more freedom to spread out freely in all directions.
2. Use a topic, title, image, or picture in the middle of the page or screen as a central idea.
3. Use colors throughout the mind map to add energy and liveliness. Color makes keywords more memorable.
4. Add topics and subtopics with keywords. Connect main branches to the central image.
5. Use curved branches to connect topics and subtopics to keep the brain stimulated.
6. Use one keyword per line to allow the mind map greater power and flexibility.
7. Use images throughout—a picture is worth a thousand words (Figure 2.2).

Mind maps are read clockwise, starting at the top of the page. "Starting at the top of the page; subtopics read from top to bottom. The most important factor is that all the information is stored on one sheet of paper or screen" (Dickinson, 2016, p. 26).

FIGURE 2.2

Example of a Mind Map

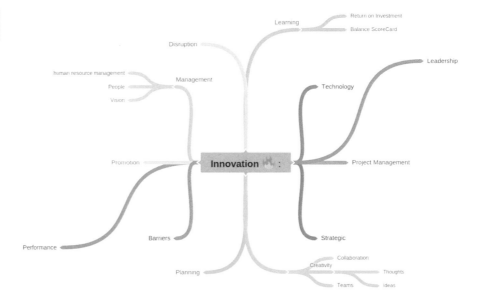

KEY TOOLS OF WRITING AND RESEARCH *A Guide for the Student Writer*

MIND-MAPPING SOFTWARE

There are many obvious advantages to using computer software versus hand-drawn maps when mind mapping, such as the ability to use hyperlink information or notes. Moreover, mind mapping apps make it easier to modify and integrate with other software like Microsoft Word. Most software companies offer easy-to-create templates with real-time collaboration. The disadvantages include high cost, learning the software, computer access, and map-sharing incompatibility (Tucker, Armstrong, & Massad, 2010). Most paid mind-mapping software practice a subscription-based pricing model (Figures 2.3 and 2.4).

Application	Operating system	Website
iMindMap	Windows, Mac, and web-based	imindmap.com
MindManager	Windows and Mac	www.mindjet.com
MindMeister	Online (web-based only)	www.mindmeister.com
Lucidchart	Online (web-based and Microsoft Office Integration through Microsoft Store)	www.lucidchart.com

FIGURE 2.3

Paid Mind-Mapping Software Applications

Application	Operating system	Website
Wise mapping	Online (web-based only)	www.wisemapping.com
Bubbl.us	Online (web-based only)	bubbl.us
Mindmup	Online (web-based only)	www.mindmup.com
Mind42	Online (web-based only)	mind42.com

FIGURE 2.4

Free Mind-Mapping Software Applications

Mind-mapping software can integrate with Internet browsers by use of add-ons or extensions. Remember, extensions are applications that integrate with an Internet browser to expand the functionality of the browser, which means increased interactions with web content. Add-ons help add personality to your Internet browser based on your interest and needs. Figure 2.5 provides a list of browser extensions for mind mapping.

Extension name	Internet browser	Website
SimpleMind Free	Safari	itunes.apple.com/us/app/simplemind-free/id439654198?mt=12
Coggle	Chrome	chrome.google.com/webstore/detail/coggle-collaborative-mind/hbcapocoafbfccjg-dgammadkndakcfoi?hl=en-GB
No extension	Firefox	
No extension	Edge	(Microsoft uses extensions in MS Office)

FIGURE 2.5

Internet Browser Extensions for Mind Mapping

To integrate mind mapping with Microsoft Word:

1. Open MS Word, PowerPoint, or Excel, or go to the Microsoft Store.
2. Enter "mind map" into the search feature.
3. Choose and install application options. You may have to pay or sign up for a free trial.
4. Create and insert your first diagram (Figures 2.6 and 2.6.1).

Figure 2.6 Access to Microsoft Store through Microsoft Word

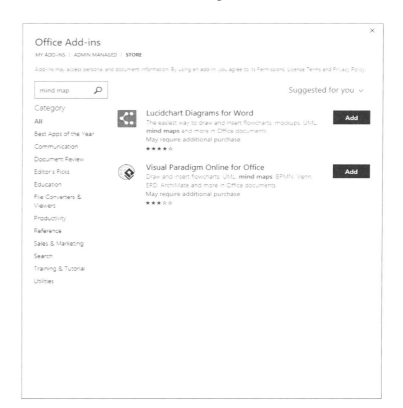

Freewriting

Freewriting allows for word association by hopping from one idea to another. It captures words, thoughts, or images that dart through one's mind. The writer explores and associates ideas by jumping from one to the next. Freewriting is

KEY TOOLS OF WRITING AND RESEARCH *A Guide for the Student Writer*

an introspective process. The freewriting experience breaks down psychological barriers, opening the mind to the possibilities of discovering hidden knowledge. Freewriting is considered a thought-starting process that helps students eliminate the fear of writing and assists in starting a new writing assignment.

The purpose of freewriting is to generate ideas before students experience the other stages of the writing process. Freewriting is effective when attempting to write paragraphs or essays. The goal is to compose as rapidly as possible to take words from the student's head to the paper. It can be a helpful tool for students who are anxious about writing or for those who are slow writers (Fox & Suhor, 1986). Additionally, it is better for students who are creative and need a free and open style. Remember not to evaluate or comment on the words that flow. These words are not to be edited or critiqued; analyzing will happen later in the writing process.

HOW TO FREEWRITE

1. Write nonstop for 10 to 15 minutes.
2. Do not be concerned about grammar, spelling, or editing.
3. Write as much as possible, and write quickly without stopping.
4. Write ideas as they come to mind. Write down everything that comes to mind. If you run out of ideas, then write anything, even if it appears silly (Clouse, 2006).
5. Once finished, look for patterns in your writing. You will likely find a topic.

Please remember that freewriting is not considered the first draft of your paper. Consider freewriting as clearing your head of ideas about your topic that will assist you in creating your first draft (Gabbrielli, 2013).

Thesis Statement

A **thesis statement** is the beacon of light within your paper. Everything you write goes to support, explain, or prove it. The thesis statement is a point of view that is arguable, persuasive, or reminiscent of a major claim that can be defended with scholarly evidence. The thesis statement is the purpose of the paper, the "why" or "how." In formal academic papers and research papers, the thesis statement is placed near the end of the introduction, and when writing the conclusion, the thesis is usually restated.

thesis statementa

A point of view that is arguable, persuasive, or a reminder of a major claim that can be defended with scholarly evidence. The thesis statement is the purpose of the paper, the "why" or "how."

A good thesis should:

- Focus on one central point or issue
- Assist in organizing the paper
- Limit **scope creep** within the paper. Scope creep is going outside the boundaries of the writing project. The thesis statement indicates parameters of the project because it is the purpose of the paper.

scope creep

Going outside the boundaries of the writing project.

- Give the preview of the paper, just like a movie preview. McWhorter (2016) believed that the thesis statement is a promise to your reader of the information yet to come in the paper).

Rhetorical Modes

rhetorical mode

How a writer communicates through language and writing. Which mode the writer chooses depends on his or her purpose for writing.

In simple terms, **rhetorical modes** are how we communicate through language and writing. The choice of mode depends on what type of essay is being developed. The purpose of the essay is also a key factor. A variety of rhetorical modes can be used within one essay. Mixing modes occurs when the writer needs to express further clarity (McLean, 2011). All tools for rhetorical modes require brainstorming. The type of brainstorming activity used depends on the rhetorical mode. Choosing a rhetorical mode makes brainstorming a more structured event. Figure 2.7 lists each rhetorical mode and the structured analytical tools that assist in writing and communication.

FIGURE 2.7

Rhetorical Modes Table with Matching Analytic Tool

Use	Rhetorical Mode	Structured Analytical Tools
To tell a story or express feelings	Narration — Chronological order	• Storyboarding • Chain of events chart • Smartphone
	Description — Spatial order — Sequential order	
To explain or express concepts, ideas, or meaning	Exemplification and illustration	Scholarly literature, stories, case studies
	Classification and division	Affinity diagram
	Process analysis	Process mapping, also called flowcharting
	Definition	Dictionary and scholarly articles
	Cause and effect	Ishikawa diagram, also called cause-and-effect diagram or fishbone diagram
To encourage change	Compare and contrast — Problem/solution — Advantages/disadvantages — Pros and cons — Strengths/weakness — Opportunities/threats	• Force-field analysis • Pros, cons, faults, and fixes analysis • SWOTT analysis
	Persuasion or argumentation	• Argument map • SWOTT analysis

KEY TOOLS OF WRITING AND RESEARCH *A Guide for the Student Writer*

NARRATION

Everyone loves a good story. We all have our favorite movies where we sit around with friends and rehash what happened. Some stories we tell over and over again. Narration is what allows the writer to send a message and transmit a story in the order of how it happened. Narrative events use chronological order to tell a story.

Storyboarding

Storyboarding is the art of the narrative. Storyboards are tools that assist the writer in telling the story in segments. Often used in writing for movies and television, storyboards align directly with writing a narrative essay. Using visuals can assist with simplifying the process of storytelling. Storyboarding allows the writer to draw out the story frame by frame, then write what each frame represents. With each frame in the storyboard, organization is being created where a story is told in a particular **sequence**. Storyboarding allows the plot, character, content, and message to emerge in key frames (Figure 2.8) (Andersson, Öberg, & Ericksson, 2011).

storyboarding

A tool that assists the writer in telling a story in segments.

sequence

Events or processes told in a particular order. First, second, third, and fourth is a form of sequence.

Story Name:_____
Location:_____
Time of Year:_____
Date:_____

FIGURE 2.8

Storyboarding Example

Event/Scene 1
Draw, place a picture, or describe the visual/action in the block.

Event/Scene 2
Draw, place a picture, or describe the visual/action in the block.

Event/Scene 3
Draw, place a picture, or describe the visual/action in the block.

- Write dialog or story of each drawing or picture
- What actions took place
- Describe feeling at the time the action took place

- Write dialog or story of each drawing or picture
- What actions took place
- Describe feeling at the time the action took place

- Write dialog or story of each drawing or picture
- What actions took place
- Describe feeling at the time the action took place

The **smartphone** is a great tool to assist with storyboarding because pictures are easily taken and stored, and notes can be written immediately. Smartphones can be an excellent tool for writing and learning.

smartphone

Handheld personal computer, telephone, and camera with Internet access.

Chain of events chart

A **chain of events** chart is a tool that assists in writing a story according to the sequence of events. When writing a personal narrative, events can sometimes become cloudy. This tool helps clarify and organize memory. Just like storyboarding, pictures and drawings are useful when trying to remember a sequence of events (Figure 2.9).

chain of events

Tool that assists in writing a story according to the sequence of events.

FIGURE 2.9

Chain of Events or Sequence
Chart

First

Then

Next

Afterward

Last

Smartphone

A smartphone is a helpful tool in this process. For example, most smartphones have a story feature. Stories can be created automatically based on faces, time, and locations of pictures and videos. Another great feature is the Global Positioning System (GPS) metadata on each picture. GPS data will give you the time and location of where each picture was taken. Not only can you create a story, but you can also create a timeline (Figure 2.10).

DESCRIPTION

Description allows the writer to transmit the physical characteristics of an object or person. Objects can be described using diagrams, pictures, drawings, tables, and figures. When describing a person, a writer will usually use sight, sound, smell, emotions, or reactions (a response to an attitude, situation, or event).

FIGURE 2.10

Example of Smartphone Auto Story Application

By going into the Gallery Settings, you will be able to access your phone's story feature.

East pop/Shutterstock.com

EXEMPLIFICATION OR ILLUSTRATION

Exemplification, also called illustration, uses examples to explain concepts and ideas. Effective illustrations use examples to support topics through evidence, given in the form of scholarly litera-ture, historical events, field experts, statistics, or current events (Figure 2.11).

Government agency	US government data and statistics websites	Description
US Government Portal	www.usa.gov	One-stop portal to all government agencies
Census Bureau	www.census.gov	Statistics
Bureau of Labor Sta-tistics	www.bls.gov	US agency that collects facts on labor
Bureau of Economic Analysis	www.bea.gov	US economic statistics
National Archive	www.archives.gov	US agency for history
Library of Congress	www.loc.gov	US Library
Federal Statistical System	www.usa.gov/statistics	Locating data, facts, and statistics from the US fed-eral statistical system

FIGURE 2.11

Government Websites Used for Statistical Evidence

CLASSIFICATION AND DIVISION

Classification sorts ideas and topics into categories. Division breaks down topics into subtopics for increased understanding. The purpose of classification and

affinity diagram

Assists the writer in categorizing and identifying relationships between ideas.

division is to make brainstorming a manageable process. An **affinity diagram** is a prewriting brainstorming strategy that assists with classification and division.

Affinity diagram

An affinity diagram assists the writer in categorizing and identifying relationships between ideas. It is a quality-management tool used in business to assist with organizing a large number of ideas into logical groupings. In fact, it is a classic tool to assist in group problem-solving and figuring out new relationships. This can be a great brainstorming activity for learning teams (Figure 2.12) (MacDonald, 2001; Tague, 2005).

FIGURE 2.12

Example of an Affinity Diagram

Affinity diagrams are usually created after brainstorming has taken place. The best way to create one is to use sticky notes to write down ideas. Below are the steps to creating an affinity diagram:

1. After ideas are written down, randomly place notes on table or board.
2. Look for ideas that can be grouped together by key themes.
3. Create a summary heading for each group and arrange the ideas within the group. This is called affinitizing.
4. Keep repeating this process until all sticky notes are beneath a category.
5. If there is a stray note, then that could possibly be an idea that does not belong or that needs further exploration.
6. Once all the categories are in place, the writer has the beginnings of an outline. Each category is a main topic and the ideas are the supporting topics.

PROCESS ANALYSIS

Process analysis explains how to do a particular procedure, job, or task that is linked in a particular sequence. "Generally, processes involve combinations of people, machines, tools, techniques, materials, and improvements in a defined series of steps or actions" (National Institute of Standards and Technology, 2015, p. 52). A classic example of a process is a recipe for a cake. In a recipe, step-by-step instructions are given to make a good cake. Process analysis is used for understanding instructions and clarifying tasks. Analysis and mapping are **structured analytic techniques** used in many academic and business disciplines.

structured analytic technique

Tools used to organize and structure the thought process to encourage problem-solving.

PROCESS MAPPING

A process lists procedures step by step to solve a problem. In the computer science and mathematics universe, listing procedures step by step is called an algorithm, which is used for problem-solving and programming. Process analysis is one of the rhetorical modes of writing where the writer explains how to do a particular action step by step. To visualize the process, a process map or **flowchart** is drawn after the step-by-step actions are written. A **process map** is a graphical representation of major steps and decisions in a process. In business, process mapping is used for process improvement, process planning, or process documentation (Figure 2.13) (Tague, 2005).

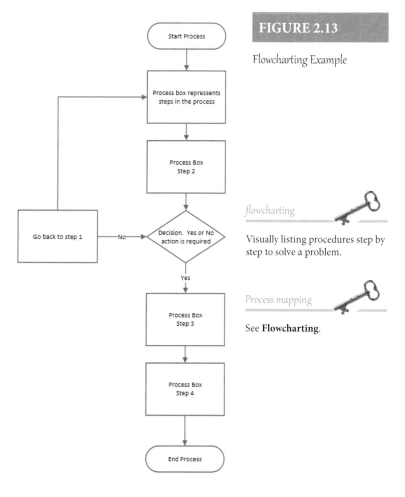

FIGURE 2.13

Flowcharting Example

flowcharting

Visually listing procedures step by step to solve a problem.

Process mapping

See **Flowcharting**.

DEFINITION

A definition explains the meaning of a word. Most students use online dictionaries to obtain definitions. Dictionaries can be a good starting point; the use of scholarly literature is another source to define words. An operational definition is a definition the writer uses to explain a particular concept. This is important in writing so the reader will have the same understanding of a term. To create an operational definition, the writer must research several scholarly sources, use a good dictionary, under-

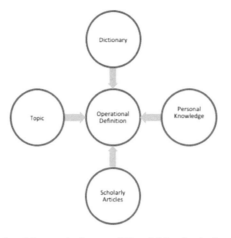

stand their topic, and mix it with their personal knowledge to create a new meaning for the work being written. Operational definitions are often used in industry to avoid ambiguous terminology and language. By using the same terms, everyone will understand without question during a project or event (Baker, 2015). For example, in the information technology industry, the term "crash" or "crashing" has a different meaning than in the healthcare industry. "Crash" in the information technology industry means software or hardware failure. In the healthcare industry, it means a person going through a drug withdrawal. When writing a definition, consider your audience. This is why it is important to research the correct definition (Figure 2.14).

CAUSE AND EFFECT

cause and effect

Also known as the Ishikawa or fishbone diagram. Allows people to organize thoughts about problems and what may be causing them.

Cause and effect explains why an outcome occurred. When brainstorming with cause and effect, the problem is the effect, or the symptom. What are the possible causes for the symptoms? For example, a business may be experiencing low sales. Low sales is the effect (symptom), so what are the causes of low sales? This may be a defective product, lack of interest, or lack of training. Cause and effect is a common tool that is used in business and quality management.

Fishbone diagram

fishbone

See Cause-and-effect diagram.

Ishikawa diagram

See **Cause-and-effect diagram**.

The **fishbone** diagram is also known as the cause-and-effect diagram or **Ishikawa diagram**. It was created by Kaoru Ishikawa to illustrate the causes of a decision, problem, or event. The words and ideas that extend from the ribs of the fish are the possible causes of the problem. A fishbone diagram allows people to organize thoughts about problems and what may be causing them (Lerner & Lerner, 2006). It is a systematic way to structure and analyze data related to solving a quality problem. The key to generating ideas for the fishbone is to ask, "Why does this happen?" (Figure 2.15)

The fishbone diagram can be used as an individual or team project. To develop a fishbone analysis, perform the following steps:

1. Write the problem or topic at the head of the fish.
2. Brainstorm the possible causes of the problem. These could be technology, people (manpower), equipment, processes, environment, or resources.
3. Write the possible causes in the would-be "ribs" or categories of the fish.

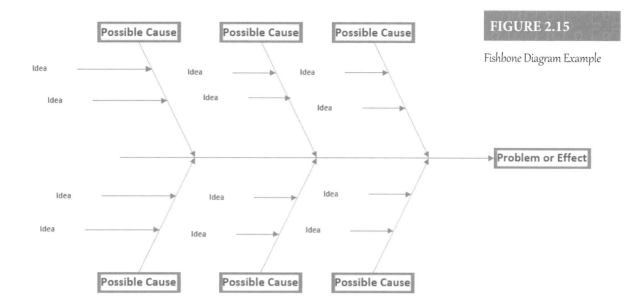

FIGURE 2.15

Fishbone Diagram Example

4. Brainstorm again how to generate more ideas for the possible causes. Ask, "Why does this happen?" This will generate sub-causes.
5. By asking "Why does this happen" generate sub-causes.
6. Purify the fishbone. Once finished generating ideas, then begin to prioritize and research each idea for relevance.
7. Develop an action plan for writing. The causes will become the outline of the paper.

The power of the fishbone session has three main phases: (1) brainstorming, (2) prioritizing, and (3) development. Phase one and two allow the user to create and organize. Phase three allows for implementation. The implementation phase is outlining and writing your cause-and-effect essay.

COMPARE AND CONTRAST

Compare and contrast illustrates similarities and differences between people, places, concepts, or ideas. Other forms of a compare-and-contrast essay are:

- Problem/solution
- Advantages/disadvantages
- Pros/cons
- Strengths/weaknesses
- Opportunities/threats

When comparing and contrasting, look for meaningful links between subjects. Tools that can help in writing compare-and-contrast papers are force-field analysis; pros, cons, faults, and fixes analysis; and SWOTT analysis.

Force-field analysis

force-field analysis

A tool that allows the writer to list items for or against a particular topic.

A force field is a tool that allows the writer to list items for or against a particular topic. This tool is good to use when considering the factors that influence a situation (Heuer & Pherson, 2011). It is often used in change management. When writing a paper on pros/cons or advantages/disadvantages, force-field analysis assists the writer with creating topics and organizing their essay. The difference between this kind of analysis and just making a list for or against a topic is that force-field analysis adds value for each item or against each item. Once the items are weighted, then the writer knows which topics are of importance (Figure 2.16) (Hill, 2012).

FIGURE 2.16

Force-Field Analysis

Forces for/driving forces	Score	Proposed topic of change	Forces against/ restraining forces	Score
Increases tax revenue	5		Considered gateway drug	5
Boost in economy	3		Decreases mental health	4
Supports public program	2		Addictive	2
Medicinal use to treat diseases	4	Legalization of Marijuana	Increase in accidents and public safety	1
Total	14		Total	12

Force-field analysis looks at the interaction of the opposing forces. This tool may be used as an individual or group activity. To develop a force-field analysis, the following must be performed:

1. First, define the problem.
2. List the main forces that impact the issue in discussion.
3. Divide the list into driving forces and restraining forces.
4. For each force, assign a number of intensity, 1 through 5 (five being the most intense and one being the least intense). For teams, each member should take a vote on each topic, then add each topic to come up with a specific number. For example, if there are five members, take a vote on the topic "increase tax revenue" then place the added number in the box.
5. Add values in each column to determine which is more important.
6. Review to see if any of the driving or restraining forces cancel each other out.

Once completed, the writer now has an important pros-and-cons list from which to write. For a team, the group now knows whether the driving forces are more important than the restraining forces for team consensus. Additionally, the list can now become an outline for research.

Pros, cons, faults, and fixes analysis

Most students have heard of creating a list of **pros and cons** for new ideas. The pros are listed on one side and the cons on the other. The **pros, cons, faults, and fixes analysis**, however, is a decision-making tool. It also prevents the writer from making a quick decision and coming to a conclusion too soon. The technique requires the writer to make a list of pros and cons. Next, look for any faults. A fault is an unrealistic argument. Look at the pros and ask the question, what is unrealistic about the pros list? These will become the fault of the pros list. After looking at pros, review the cons list to identify any fixes. Fixes are "any argument or plan that would neutralize or minimize a con" (Heuer & Pherson, 2011, p. 284). Any faults or fixes allow the opportunity for research, investigation, and removal of barriers (Figure 2.17).

pros and cons

List of reasons for or against an issue.

Pros, cons, faults, and fixes

List of reasons for or against an issue, including a proposed solution for each pro and con.

Topic/Problem/Argument			
Faults	**Pros**	**Cons**	**Fixes**
(What is unrealistic about Pro 1)	Pro 1	Con 1	(What would neutralize or minimize Con 1)
Fault Pro 2	Pro 2	Con 2	Con Fix 2
Fault Pro 3	Pro 3	Con 3	Con Fix 3
Fault Pro 4	Pro 4	Con 4	Con Fix 4
Fault Pro 4	Pro 5	Con 5	Con Fix 5

FIGURE 2.17

Pros, Cons, Faults, and Fixes Analysis

1. Create a standard pro/con list based on a topic, problem, or argument.
2. Review the list for repetition or overlap.
3. Next, write down the faults of each pro. Is there are any reason why the pro is unreasonable or would not work?
4. Look at all of your cons and write down what would fix, eliminate, or minimize each one.
5. Research each pro and con to ensure it is a viable research choice. List the research information you find. This information can be used at a later time.
6. Once the list is fully completed, you can decide which pros and cons are suitable for your essay.

PERSUASION OR ARGUMENTATION

Argumentation allows the writer to take a stance on a position for a belief, argument, or debate. The position is supported by persuasion, which will influence the reader through facts and evidence. Both argumentation and persuasion rely on the intent of the writer. A writer with a good intent will present a balanced argument.

Argument map

An **argument map** is a critical tool in the development of an argument essay. "Argument mapping is similar to other mapping activities such as mind mapping and concept mapping, but focuses on the logical, evidential relationships among propositions" (Van Gelder, 2013, p. 51). The argument map assists in thought organization, clarification of reasoning, communication, and the development of an outline. Another benefit is that it aids the writer in discovering unrealistic assumptions and gaps in knowledge where no research is available to present as evidence (Figure 2.18) (Heuer & Pherson, 2011; Reasoning Lab, 2018). Argument mapping can be a group or solitary activity. To develop an argument map, the following must be performed:

1. Begin with an argument, judgment, statement, or potential decision to be accepted or rejected.
2. List reasons for or against the argument.
3. For each reason, list evidence.
4. For each piece of evidence, find literature that supports it.

By following these steps, the writer is creating scholarly support for the argument. In addition, the writer is drafting a basic outline for their paper.

FIGURE 2.18

Argument Map

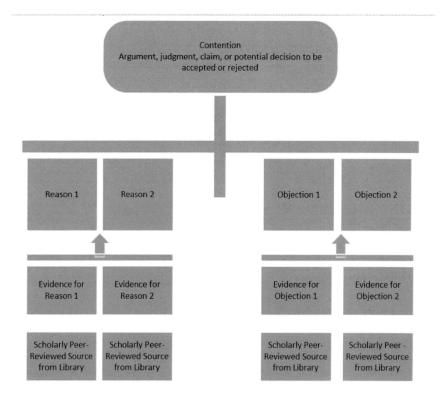

KEY TOOLS OF WRITING AND RESEARCH *A Guide for the Student Writer*

SWOTT analysis

FIGURE 2.19

SWOTT is an acronym for Strengths, Weaknesses, Opportunities, Threats, and Trends. Traditionally, this strategic planning tool is used to analyze an organiza-

SWOTT Analysis

tion internally and externally to identify factors that would help or harm the organization. In addition, the SWOTT tool is used to identify competitors. SWOTT is helpful in providing a strong, persuasive argument for making a decision (Figure 2.19). Students who are business majors will become very familiar with this tool (Heuer & Pherson, 2011; Maruca, 2008).

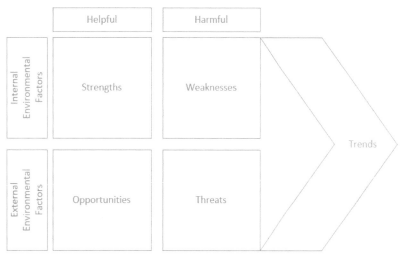

Strengths are internal assets and fortitude that will allow the argument, process, or organization goal achievement.

Weaknesses are internal vulnerabilities that will prevent a positive outcome.

Opportunities are a set of conditions that will result in a positive outcome. What are the external opportunities that will allow the argument, process, or organization goal achievement?

SWOTT analysis

Strengths, weaknesses, opportunity, threats, and trends. Helpful in providing a strong argument for making a decision.

Threats are a set of external conditions that impact decision making and result in a negative outcome. They can be political, environmental, social, cultural, or technological (PEST) factors that impact an argument, process, or goal.

Trends take a look at the future and tie the SWOTT together. When writing trends, prediction is a key word. Identifying trends requires further research and assessment because you are looking at outside sources to aid in forecasting. Forecasting involves reviewing strengths, weaknesses, opportunities, and threats to foresee how these factors will affect an argument, a process, or an organization's goal achievement.

Summary

Prewriting is an important step after you gather your writing assets. The prewriting process starts you on the journey of discovery, which includes generating ideas, finding research, and using the correct analytical tools. The correct analytical tools will allow for structured brainstorming, which improves the efficiency and effectiveness of your writing and produces more expedient results. This chapter matches rhetorical modes with structured analytical tools to enhance the experience and effectiveness of the prewriting process. By using structured brainstorming with rhetorical modes, writing can be precise.

Key Terms

Affinity diagram
Argument map
Brainstorming
Cause and effect
Chain of events
Convergent thinking
Divergent thinking
Fishbone

Flowcharting
Force-field analysis
Freewriting
Ishikawa diagram
Mind mapping
Prewriting
Pros and cons
Process mapping

Pros, cons, fault, and
    fixes analysis
Research
Rhetorical mode
Scope creep
Sequence
Smartphone
Storyboarding

Structured analytical
    techniques
SWOTT analysis
Thesis statement
Topic

Review Questions

1. Explain the importance of research in academic writing.
2. Identify the steps in choosing a topic.
3. Compare and contrast individual brainstorming with team brainstorming.
4. Explain the difference between divergent and convergent thinking.
5. What is an Internet browser extension, and how is it used?
6. Identify and explain the different brainstorming techniques.
7. Define structured analytical techniques, and explain how they are used with rhetorical modes.
8. How are rhetorical modes used to communicate?
9. Identify the requirements of a good thesis statement.
10. How can a smartphone be used in writing?
11. List the steps in freewriting.
12. Describe the steps in storyboarding.
13. What is a chain-of-events chart, and why is it used in writing?
14. List and describe the tools needed for effective writing.
15. Identify websites used for statistical evidence.
16. What is an affinity diagram, and how is it used in brainstorming?
17. Define process analysis.
18. Identify a process, then create a flowchart for the process.
19. What are the different names for the Ishikawa diagram?
20. Identify and describe the tools used to write a pros and cons essay.
21. What is an operational definition, and how is it used in an essay?
22. Explain the components of an operational definition.
23. Identify and explain the three main phases of the fishbone diagram.
24. List the steps to creating an argument map.
25. Summarize the essential elements of a SWOTT analysis.

References

Andersson, J., Oberg, A., & Eriksson, Y. (2011). The use of storyboard to capture experiences. In *DS 68-10: Proceedings of the 18th International Conference on Engineering Design (ICED 11), Impacting Society through Engineering Design, Vol. 10: Design Methods and Tools pt. 2, Lyngby/Copenhagen, Denmark, 15.-19.08. 2011* (pp. 331–340). Copenhagen, Denmark: The Design Society. Retrieved from https://www.designsociety.org/publication/30764/the+use+of+storyboard+to+capture+experiences

Badke, W. (2011). *Research strategies: Finding your way through the information fog* (4th ed.). Bloomington, IN: iUniverse.

Baker, C. L. (2015). *Channel of distribution restructuring: A cross-sectional time series study of Chrysler, Ford, and General Motors from 2006 to 2011 in the united states* (Order No. 3682569). Available from ProQuest Dissertations & Theses Global. (1658143902).

Budd, J. W. (2004). Mind maps as classroom exercises. *Journal of Economic Education, 35*(1), 35–46. Retrieved from https://doi.org/10.3200/JECE.35.1.35-46.

Buzan, T. (2002). *How to Mind Map: The Thinking Tool That Will Change Your Life* (1st printing edition). London, England: Thorsons.

Buzan, T., & Buzan, B. (1996). *The mind map book: How to use radiant thinking to maximize your brain's untapped potential* (reprint edition). New York: Plume.

Central Intelligence Agency. (2009). *A Tradecraft Primer: Structured Analytic Techniques for Improving Intelligence Analysis.* Washington, DC: CIA Sherman Kent School. Retrieved from https://www.cia.gov/library/center-for-the-study-of-intelligence/csi-publications/books-and-monographs/Tradecraft%20Primer-apr09.pdf

Chan, W. (2004). *The effectiveness of using mind mapping skills in enhancing secondary one and secondary four students' writing in a CMI school.* The University of Hong Kong, Hong Kong. Retrieved from http://www.airitilibrary.com/Publication/alDetailedMesh?docid=U0029-1812201200004542

Clouse, B. F. (2006). *The student writer* (7th ed.). New York: McGraw-Hill.

Davies, M. (2011). Concept mapping, mind mapping and argument mapping: what are the differences and do they matter? *Higher Education; Dordrecht, 62*(3), 279–301. Retrieved from https://doi.org/10.1007/s10734-010-9387-6

Dickinson, I. (2016). "Mind maps": helping from pedagogy to packing. *Trends in Urology & Men's Health, 7*(4), 25–27. Retrieved from https://doi.org/10.1002/tre.534

Dutt, M. (2015). Adding value to projects using mind maps. *Journal of Creating Value, 1*(2), 221–234. Retrieved from https://doi.org/10.1177/2394964315602412

Farrand, P., Hussain, F., & Hennessy, E. (2002). The efficacy of the 'mind map' study technique. *Medical Education, 36*(5), 426–431. Retrieved from http://onlinelibrary.wiley.com/doi/10.1046/j.1365-2923.2002.01205.x/full

Fox, D., & Suhor, C. (1986). ERIC/RCS report: Limitations of free writing. *The English Journal, 75*(8), 34–36. Retrieved from https://doi.org/10.2307/819077

Gabbrielli, R., (2013). Using free writing in the classroom. *Modern English Teacher, 22*(4), 17–21.

Heuer, R. J., & Pherson, R. H. (2011). *Structured analytic techniques for intelligence analysis.* Washington, DC: CQ Press College.

Hill, S. D. (Ed.). (2012). Strategy implementation. In *Encyclopedia of Management* (7th ed., pp. 946–950). Detroit, MI: Gale. Retrieved from http://link.galegroup.com/apps/doc/CX4016600285/GVRL?u=gtechclg&sid=GVRL&xid=21f175b2

JSTOR Labs. (2017). *Topicgraph.* Retrieved from https://labs.jstor.org/topicgraph/about

Lerner, K. L., & Lerner, B. W. (Eds.). (2006). Plots and diagrams. In *Real-Life Math* (Vol. 2, pp. 404–415). Detroit, MI: Gale. Retrieved from http://link.galegroup.com/apps/doc/CX3447900070/GVRL?u=gtechclg&sid=GVRL&xid=d284ae25

Litchfield, R. C. (2008). Brainstorming reconsidered: A goal-based view. *Academy of Management Review, 33*(3), 649–668. Retrieved from https://doi.org/10.5465/AMR.2008.32465708

MacDonald, D. (2001). Affinity diagrams: Organizing mountains of data. In M. Hiebert & B. Klatt (Eds.), *The encyclopedia of leadership: A practical guide to popular leadership theories and techniques* (pp. 227–230). New York: McGraw-Hill Professional. Retrieved from http://link.galegroup.com/apps/doc/CX3475700082/GVRL?u=gtechclg&sid=GVRL&xid=04cbf977.

Maruca, R. F. (Ed.). (2008). SWOT Analysis. In *The Way We Work: An Encyclopedia of Business Culture* (Vol. 2, pp. 343–345). Westport, CT: Greenwood Press. Retrieved from http://link.galegroup.com/apps/doc/CX2457800125/GVRL?u=gtechclg&sid=GVRL&xid=0778e372

McLean, S. (2011). *Writing for success* (1st ed.). Boston, MA: Flat World Knowledge, Inc.

McWhorter, K. T. (2016). *Successful college writing* (6th ed.). Boston, MA: Bedford/St. Martin's.

National Institute of Standards and Technology. (2015). *2015–2016 Baldrige Excellence Framework (Education)* (Publication) (p. 68). Gaithersburg, MD: US Department of Commerce. Retrieved from https://www.nist.gov/baldrige/publications/baldrige-excellence-framework/education#ed

Osborn, A. F. (1957). *Applied imagination: Principles and procedures of creative problem-solving* (Rev. ed.). New York: C. Scribner's Sons.

Reasoning Lab. (2018). *Argument mapping* [Corporate]. Retrieved from https://www.reasoninglab.com/argument-mapping/

Tague, N. R. (2005). *The quality toolbox* (2nd ed.). Milwaukee, WI: ASQ Quality Press.

Tucker, J. M., Armstrong, G. R., & Massad, V. J. (2010). Profiling a mind map user: A descriptive appraisal. *Journal of Instructional Pedagogies, 2*. Retrieved from http://eric.ed.gov/?id=EJ1056389

Van Gelder, T. (2013). Argument mapping. In H. Pashler (Ed.), *Encyclopedia of the mind* (Vol. 1, pp. 51–52). Thousand Oaks, CA: SAGE Publications, Inc.

CHAPTER 3

Outlining

Chapter Learning Objectives:

- Identify and explain the real purpose of an outline.
- Discuss logical orderly thinking.
- Discuss the advantages of an outline.
- Define and create a table of contents from an outline.
- Define headings and heading levels.
- Define and discuss outlining as a strategy.

The Real Purpose of an Outline

When asked to define strategy, few people would think of an outline. **Strategy** is a plan, pattern, position, perspective, and ploy created to achieve a goal. Outlining is the strategic portion of writing. Strategy sets direction, focuses effort, provides consistency, and defines organization within a paper. It provides opportunity for reflection and awareness. Outlining is a strategy because it is a continual process (Mintzberg, Lampel, &, Anhalstrand, 2005; Pearce & Robinson, 2010). It is a planning strategy that positively influences writing and creates patterns of consistent behavior. An outline decreases the mental gymnastics and emotional trauma of writing (Figure 3.1) (De Smet, Brand-Gruwel, Broekkamp, & Kirschner, 2012).

Outlining is a language skill; it clarifies the thought process and eliminates unnecessary topics that could pollute conversation and transmission of thought to the reader (Taylor, 2012). By doing this, it allows the writer to make a position known and take a stand on a matter of importance. Outlining allows the writer to present a unique perspective, provoking thoughts and ideas within the reader. Finally, outlines are a tactic, a ploy, to allow maneuverability within the writing framework. Most studies illustrate that using outlining as a strategy leads to improving the quality of written text.

strategy

A plan, pattern, position, perspective, and ploy created to achieve a goal.

FIGURE 3.1

Outline as a Strategy Road Map

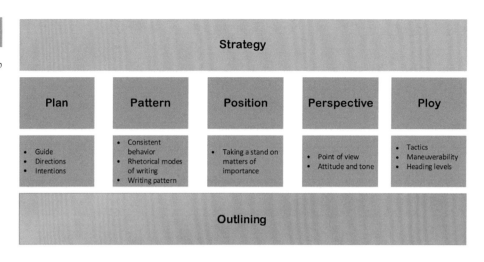

Two Types of Outlines

INFORMAL OUTLINE

Also known as a scratch outline because you are more likely to freewrite. Uses a simple list of main points by using keywords and phrases.

Informal outlines are also known as scratch outlines because you are more likely to freewrite, question, or make lists. Scratch outlines allow the writer to collect ideas and list key phrases or words for further refinement. These keywords or phrases are created by brainstorming or asking yourself why your thesis statement is valid. The informal outline assists a writer in planning research and organizing ideas. Unlike a formal outline, it does not require a formal structure such as parallelism. The form of an informal outline is at the writer's discretion.

FORMAL OUTLINE

A structured, detailed outline with main points (topics) and supporting points (subtopics) that have parallel structure.

A **formal outline** is a structured, detailed outline that has main points (topics) and supporting points (subtopics) that have parallel structure. Parallelism is "repetition of key terms and of sentence patterns" (Ogden, 1948, p. 156). Parallel structures coordinate topics. Each topic and subtopic has the same level of importance. In addition, if you outline in complete sentences, then your entire outline must be in complete sentences.

Formal outlines can be topic or sentence outlines. Topic outlines use keywords or phrases to communicate in concrete form and language. This will give the reader insight into information in a way that is easily understandable and digestible. Again, topic outlines are most useful when there are parallel points (Chase, 1949).

Once your formal outline is created, it becomes a blueprint to help you achieve a document that is well organized and supported by research. In formal outlining, there cannot be a I without a II, nor can you have an A without a B. When an object is divided, it is always divided into two or more parts. For example, if you divide a cake into parts, you will no longer have one cake; it will be at least two parts. When dividing topics into subtopic, remember that there must be at least two subparts or topics (Ogden, 1948). A formal outline illustrates research, planning, and thought.

Advantages of an Outline

SUPPORTS THESIS STATEMENT

A well-structured outline supports your thesis statement (Thomas, 2004). If it does not, then you are discussing two different topics and you are not providing evidentiary support for your argument. Basically, you are not proving your argument because you are not discussing the actual topic.

IDENTIFIES MAIN IDEAS

The **main idea** consists of the most important points about a paragraph. Outlining assists students in creating the main ideas within the paper, which produces a clear hierarchical sequence and indicates relationships between topics and supporting details. By indicating the relationships between ideas, the readers are able to analyze the major and minor points within the paper and determine how those points are connected. Outlining enables linking and connection of ideas. "Writing from the outline helps preserve the logic of the research itself. An outline identifies main ideas, defines subordinate ideas, helps you discipline your writing and avoid tangential excursions, and helps you notice omissions. In an outline, you can also identify subheadings that will be used in the article itself" (American Psychological Association [APA], 2010, p. 70).

main idea

The most important point about a paragraph.

SUPPORTS LOGICAL AND ORDERLY THINKING

Outlining is a language skill that clarifies the thought process, speaking skills, and presenting skills. A good outline guides the conversation between the writer and reader. It also eliminates unnecessary topics that pollute the conversation and transmission of thoughts to the reader. Chase (1949) stated that an outline is simply clear and logical thinking. **Logical and orderly thinking** helps writers determine the best method to develop and support arguments (Oermann, 2000). Depending on the instructions of the assignment, essays are written in some type of logical order:

logical and orderly thinking

Writers determine the best method to develop and support arguments. See **Rhetorical modes**.

- Chronological
- Spatial

- Sequential
- Compare and contrast
- Advantages and disadvantages
- Problem and solution

ORGANIZES PAPER THROUGH HEADINGS

An outline represents order in a paper. When an instructor tells you your paper lacks organization, it means you lack headings in your work. In writing, it is considered rude to give an instructor a paper that is one giant piece of text. Now, the instructor has to search within your paper and pull out where you have made your point. This type of search is called "foraging" because the instructor is hunting and digging to find where a point was discussed. Once an instructor begins foraging to find where you made your point, they uncover the most minute errors. Add headings to your paper to do the following:

- Create organization.
- Keep you on track as the writer and guide the reader through your work.
- Allow the reader insight into the document.

memory recall

The brain's ability to retrieve short- and long-term information.

Additionally, headings are used as signaling devices for subject changes (Sanford, 1968). Having headings in your document influences the reader's attention; in turn, the reader is more likely to **recall** the information being read (Lorch, Chen, & Lemarié, 2012). Your headings are topics and subtopics within your paper, which are a representation of ideas (Galbraith, Ford, Walker, & Ford, 2005). If your paper is longer than three or four pages, then headings should be used to organize the document.

CREATE TEMPLATE FOR PAPER

template

A guide or preset format for a document.

A **template** is defined as a preset format in a document. When writing according to APA guidelines, there are five levels of headings. Conversely, there are only five levels in an outline. The document heading levels directly correspond to the different levels in an outline (Figure 3.2).

Your outline becomes the headings in your paper. The headings become the template for your paper. Now once you have the template, all you have to do is write underneath each topic within your paper. Figure 3.2 illustrates how the outline becomes the template for the paper. Once you have the template, now you have organization within your work. A student can now start writing underneath each topic within the template. Now that a template has been created, there is a guide for writing.

Outline	Heading Levels in Document
I. Level One Heading	
II. Level One Heading	**Level One Heading**
A. Level Two Heading	**Level One Heading**
B. Level Two Heading	**Level Two Heading**
III. Level One Heading	**Level Two Heading**
A. Level Two Heading	**Level One Heading**
B. Level Two Heading	**Level Two Heading**
i. Level Three Heading	**Level Two Heading**
ii. Level Three Heading	**Level three heading.**
1. Level Four Heading	**Level three heading.**
2. Level Four Heading	***level four heading.***
a. Level 5 Heading	***level four heading.***
b. Level 5 Heading	*level five heading.*
	Level five heading.

FIGURE 3.2

Outline Transition to Heading Example

Universal Healthcare Debate

Rising Cost of Healthcare

Tax Debate Concerning Universal Healthcare

Federally Mandated or Universal Healthcare

Federal Stance
State Stance

Pro and Cons of Universal Healthcare

Pros of Universal Healthcare
Cons of Universal Healthcare

Universal Healthcare in Other Countries

Japan
Germany
Sweden

Conclusion

References

FIGURE 3.3

Headings in APA Format

BUILDS TABLE OF CONTENTS

table of contents

A table of contents (TOC) is a comprehensive representation of the headings and subheadings in your document.

page numbers

Number assigned to a document such as an essay or research paper. Locators to help find information in a book, journal, or article.

hyperlink

A link to another file or document location.

A **table of contents** (TOC) is a comprehensive representation of the headings and subheadings in your document (Figure 3.3). A TOC reflects the content within your paper, which represents the organization and hierarchy of your topics and subtopics (Branavan, Deshpande, & Barzilay, 2007). Understanding what a TOC represents is essential to create a table that is visually appealing. To the reader, a TOC serves as a navigational aid that allows organization of thought, structure of content, and description of text. A TOC comprises two basic elements that allow for the creation of a hierarchical structure: descriptors and locators. Descriptors are chapters or headings within the actual document. Locators are **page numbers** or **hyperlinks** used to navigate the document. By using descriptors and locators, TOCs provide insight and depth to the material being covered (Sarkar & Saund, 2008).

A TOC is created by picking up main-level and sublevel headings in the text along with the corresponding page number, according to their outline level. The headings and page numbers are placed into a table that reflects exactly what is in the document (Sullivan & Eggleston, 2006). Word processers like Microsoft Word have integrated the writing process into their program. In Microsoft Word, your outline can become your TOC. MS Word creates it by applying heading styles to the text you want to include. Review the headings and styles you programmed in chapter 1. Once you program your headings and styles, apply those to your outline (Microsoft Corporation, 2017).

Select the headings you want to include in the TOC, and then on the Home tab, click a heading style. Main topics are Heading 1 and subtopics are Heading 2 (Figure 3.4).

FIGURE 3.4

Heading Gallery

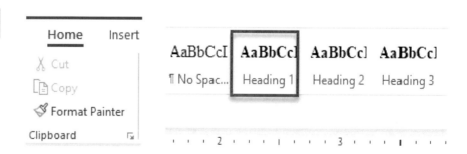

ADDING THE TABLE OF CONTENTS

Microsoft Word uses the headings in your document to build an automatic TOC that can be updated when you change the heading text, sequence, pages, or level.

1. Click where you want to insert the TOC—usually near the beginning of a document, after the title page or abstract.
2. Click **References** then **Table of Contents**, and then choose an **Automatic Table of Contents** style from the list (Figure 3.5).

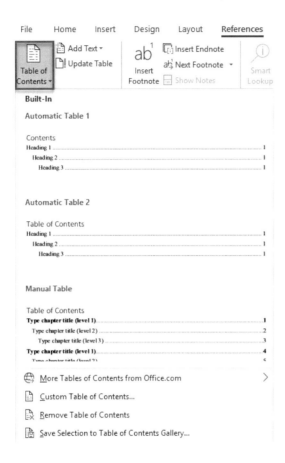

FIGURE 3.5

Table of Contents

UPDATING THE TABLE OF CONTENTS

Your TOC reflects what is in your document based on the last saved changes. If you have added more content or headings, or if the page numbers have changed, then your TOC should be updated. If a TOC is created automatically from the headings in a document, Microsoft Word can update it when those page numbers or headings change.

1. Click **References** then **Update Table**.
2. In the **Update Table of Contents** dialog box, choose **Update page numbers only** or **Update entire table**, and then click **OK** (Figure 3.6).

Note: The *American Psychological Association Publication Manual* does not provide any rules or guidance on the topic of tables of contents. Questions about tables of contents come from students or teachers who want the information to complete a class assignment. Style preferences for undergraduate writing can

FIGURE 3.6

Updating Table of Contents

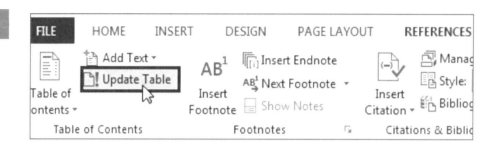

vary by discipline, university, and instructor. Students should request the preferred formatting guidelines from their instructor if a table of contents is required (APA, 2017).

IDENTIFIES MINIMUM NUMBER OF REFERENCES

Students often ask how many references are needed to complete the assignments. The outline is the key to answering this question. Count the number of main headings and subtopics within your outline, and that will give you a strong clue about the minimum number of references you need to support your work. Figure 3.7 is an outline of the topic of universal healthcare. If a student were writing this paper, they would need at least thirteen references or research sources. Why thirteen? Count the roman numerals, which are a total of six, and the subtopics (As and Bs), which are a total of seven. This gives you a total of thirteen references or sources.

Researching each topic on your outline provides you with references, improved content, and evidentiary support.

FIGURE 3.7

How to Count Minimum Number of References

I. Universal Healthcare Debate   1
II. Rising Cost of Healthcare   2
III. Tax Debate Concerning Universal Healthcare   3
IV. Federally Mandated or Universal Healthcare   4
     A. Federal Stance   5
     B. State Stance   6
V. Pro and Cons of Universal Healthcare   7
     A. Pros of Universal Healthcare   8
     B. Cons of Universal Healthcare   9
VI. Universal Healthcare in Other Countries   10
     A. Japan   11
     B. Germany   12
     C. Sweden   13
VII. Conclusion
VIII. References

IDENTIFIES KEYWORDS FOR RESEARCH

Document or subject headings are keywords, and these keywords are the beginning of your research. These headings are called "controlled vocabulary," which is necessary for smart information retrieval and providing evidence for your topic. Keywords are critical for retrieving information because they are more consistent in producing results. When using document or subject headings as keywords, students spend less time researching, which results in a more useful and meaningful search for evidence to support topics (Grey & Hurko, 2012; McCutcheon, 2009).

keyword

A word that is of importance to a concept, document, or Internet search.

ENCOURAGES EFFECTIVE TIME MANAGEMENT AND TEAM COLLABORATION

Outlining is a time-management tool. Time management is defined as using time efficiently and effectively to accomplish a task. An outline allows you to manage your time and write the paper in sections according to the topic and subtopics. Do not try to write your paper all in one sitting; use your outline as a schedule (see Figure 3.8). Writing is a less tedious process when you have a structure for writing. Outlining gives you this structure and reduces the time it takes to write. The outline below is an example of how an outline can be used to manage time when writing.

Team collaboration means working together with other people in a joint effort to achieve a common goal. Outlines can be used for collaboration and management by handing out assignments. You can assign time restraints and due dates to the outline with percentages of completion. By using the outline as a collaboration tool, it can minimize conflict in a team.

time management

Using time efficiently and effectively to accomplish a task.

outline

The strategic portion of writing. Strategy sets direction, focuses effort, provides consistency, and defines organization within a paper.

team collaboration

Working together with other people in a joint effort to achieve a common goal.

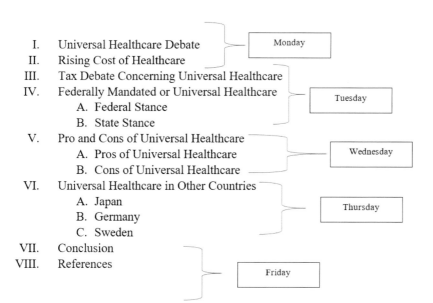

FIGURE 3.8

Using an Outline for Time Management

A well-defined outline can support the mission of the assignment (thesis statement), set goals (topics and subtopics), and secure team members' commitment (assignment of topics and subtopics) to complete the paper. Using the outline as a collaborative tool has the following advantages (Figure 3.9):

- Improves quality of group projects
- Creates team synergy
- Organizes team meetings
- Enhances group dynamics
- Promotes team learning
- Allows for virtual collaboration
- Allocates resources
- Defines leadership roles

FIGURE 3.9

An Outline Converted into a Collaborative Tool

	Tasks/topics	Team member Name	Date assigned	Due date	Resources needed for completion
I.	Universal Healthcare Debate				
II.	Rising Cost of Healthcare				
III.	Tax Debate Concerning Universal Healthcare				
IV.	Federally Mandated or Universal Healthcare				
A.	Federal Stance				
B.	State Stance				
V.	Pro and Cons of Universal Healthcare				
A.	Pros of Universal Healthcare				
B.	Cons of Universal Healthcare				
VI.	Universal Healthcare in Other Countries				
A.	Japan				
B.	Germany				
C.	Sweden				
VII.	Conclusion				
VIII.	References				

CONVERTS TO POWERPOINT PRESENTATION

Another advantage of outlining is forming the basis of your PowerPoint presentation. Microsoft Word has a command called Send to PowerPoint. This is a powerful command that works directly with Styles to connect and send your outline directly into PowerPoint. Remember, your PowerPoint is a pictorial view of your paper. A pictorial view contains pictures and text to highlight the most important points in your paper.

So how do you send your outline to PowerPoint? The Send to Microsoft PowerPoint command is hidden by default. However, you can include it in the Quick Access toolbar (Figures 3.10 to 3.10.2).

Step 1. Click on the dropdown arrow next to the Quick Access toolbar and click on **More Commands.**

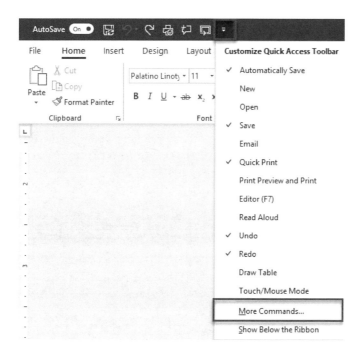

FIGURE 3.10

Send to PowerPoint Instructions

Step 2. Select *All Commands* from the available choices under *Customize the Quick Access Toolbar*. Scroll down to *Send to Microsoft PowerPoint* and add it to the Quick Access toolbar.

FIGURE 3.10.1

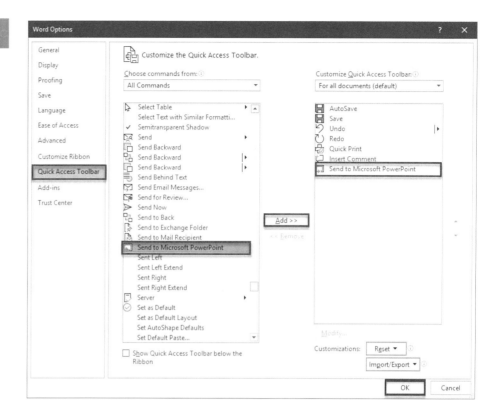

Step 3. You will see the new **Send to Microsoft PowerPoint** feature added to the remaining ones on the Quick Access toolbar.

FIGURE 3.10.2

Send to PowerPoint Instructions, Con.

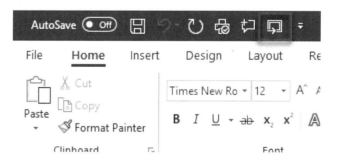

Step 4. Now you can use the heading levels formatting under Styles. PowerPoint converts heading levels in the following manner:

- Text formatted with Heading 1 becomes the title text in PowerPoint.
- Text formatted with Heading 2 is converted to first-level bullet points.
- Text formatted with Heading 3 is converted to sub-bullet points (second level).
- Text formatted with Heading 4 is converted to third-level bullet points.

AaBbCcI	AaBbCcI	AaBbCc]	AaBbCc]	AaBbCc]	AaBbCc	AaBbCcI	AaB
¶ Normal	¶ No Spac...	Heading 1	Heading 2	Heading 3	Heading 4	Heading 5	Hea

Styles

FIGURE 3.10.3

Send to PowerPoint Instructions, Con.

Universal Healthcare Debate

Rising Cost of Healthcare

FIGURE 3.10.4

Send to PowerPoint Instructions, Con

Tax Debate Concerning Universal Healthcare

Federally Mandated or Universal Healthcare
Federal Stance
State Stance

Pro and Cons of Universal Healthcare
Pros of Universal Healthcare
Cons of Universal Healthcare

Universal Healthcare in Other Countries
Japan
Germany
Sweden

Conclusion

References

Step 5. Click the **Send to PowerPoint** button in the Quick Access toolbar to quickly create the presentation slides. The outline is automatically copied or transferred to PowerPoint.

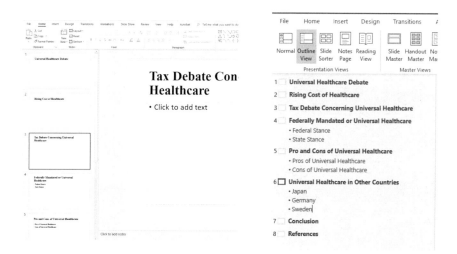

Once the outline is transferred to PowerPoint, anyone can easily see it. PowerPoint also has an outline view, which is displayed in Figure 3.10.5. The outline view allows you to see that PowerPoint is nothing but an outline with words and pictures to further convey the message of your document (Guiding Media Pvt Ltd, 2012).

Summary

The outline is the most important tool in writing. Outlining is just good strategy. View the outline as a road map to create a plan, pattern, position, perspective, and ploy within a writing assignment. Additionally, the advantages of an outline are more than strategic. An outline:

- Supports your thesis statement
- Identifies main ideas
- Supports logical thinking
- Supports organization of headings
- Creates templates
- Builds table of contents
- Identifies keywords for research
- Encourages effective time management
- Enhances team collaboration
- Transfers to PowerPoint

Key Terms

Formal outline	Logical and orderly	Outline	Table of contents
Hyperlinks	thinking	Page numbers	Team collaboration
Informal outline	Main idea	PowerPoint presentation	Template
Keywords	Memory recall	Strategy	Time management

Review Questions

1. List and describe the real purpose of an outline.
2. Why is an outline considered a strategy?
3. List and describe the advantages of outlining.
4. Summarize the importance of headings.
5. How does an outline relate to the table of contents?
6. List the steps in creating a table of contents in Microsoft Word.
7. How is an outline used to identify the minimum number of references?
8. What are the advantages of using an outline as a collaborative tool?
9. Describe how an outline is used as a time-management tool.
10. List the steps in turning an outline into a PowerPoint presentation.

References

American Psychological Association. (2010). *Publication Manual of the American Psychological Association* (6th ed.). Washington, DC: Author.

American Psychological Association. (2017). *Quick answers—formatting*. Retrieved from http://www.apastyle.org/learn/quick-guide-on-formatting.aspx

Branavan, S. R. K., Deshpande, P., & Barzilay, R. (2007). Generating a table-of-contents. In *Annual Meeting-Association for Computational Linguistics* (Vol. 45, p. 544). Retrieved from http://www.aclweb.org/old_anthology/P/P07/P07-1.pdf#page=582

Chase, N. (1949). Outlining: An aid to logical expression. *The English Journal, 38*(4), 201. Retrieved from https://doi.org/10.2307/806694

De Smet, M. J. R., Brand-Gruwel, S., Broekkamp, H., & Kirschner, P. A. (2012). Write between the lines: Electronic outlining and the organization of text ideas. *Computers in Human Behavior, 28*(6), 2107–2116. Retrieved from https://doi.org/10.1016/j.chb.2012.06.015

Galbraith, D., Ford, S., Walker, G., & Ford, J. (2005). The contribution of different components of working memory to knowledge transformation during writing. *L1-Educational Studies in Language & Literature, 5*(2), 113–145. Retrieved from https://doi.org/10.1007/s10674-005-0119-2

Grey, A., & Hurko, C. R. (2012). So you think you're an expert: Keyword searching vs. controlled subject headings. *Codex: The Journal of the Louisiana Chapter of the ACRL, 1*(4), 15–26. Retrieved from http://journal.acrlla.org/index.php/codex/article/view/47

Guiding Media Pvt Ltd. (2012, September 25). *Directly send word 2010 documents to PowerPoint 2010*. Retrieved from http://www.guidingtech.com/14966/directly-send-word-to-powerpoint-2010/

Lorch, R. F., Chen, H.-T., & Lemarié, J. (2012). Communicating headings and preview sentences in text and speech. *Journal of Experimental Psychology: Applied, 18*(3), 265–276. Retrieved from https://doi.org/10.1037/a0029547

McCutcheon, S. (2009). Keyword vs-controlled vocabulary searching: the one with the most tools wins. *The Indexer, 27*(2), 62–65.

Microsoft Corporation. (2017). *Create a table of contents in Word—Word*. Retrieved from https://support.office.com/en-us/article/Create-a-table-of-contents-in-Word-882e8564-0edb-435e-84b5-1d8552ccf0c0

Mintzberg, H., Lampel, J., & Ahlstrand, B. (2005). *Strategy safari: A guided tour through the wilds of strategic management*. New York, NY: Free Press.

Oermann, M. (2000). Refining outlining skills. *AAOHN Journal, 48*(11), 515–517.

Ogden, H. V. S. (1948). On teaching the sentence outline. *College English, 10*(3), 152–158. Retrieved from https://doi.org/10.2307/371805

Pearce, J., & Robinson, R. (2010). *Strategic management* (12th ed.). New York, NY: McGraw-Hill Education.

Sanford, B. (1968). *Heading-introduction technique*. Retrieved from http://spo.nmfs.noaa.gov/Circulars/CIRC283.pdf

Sarkar, P., & Saund, E. (2008). On the reading of tables of contents. In *The Eighth IAPR International Workshop on Document Analysis Systems* (pp. 386–393). IEEE. Retrieved from https://doi.org/10.1109/DAS.2008.87

Sullivan, K. D., & Eggleston, M. (2006). *The McGraw-Hill desk reference for editors, writers, and proofreaders* (1st ed.). New York, NY: McGraw-Hill Education.

Taylor, R. B. (2012). The joys of outlining in medical writing. *Medical Writing, 21*(3), 205–208. Retrieved from https://doi.org/10.1179/2047480612Z.00000000044

Thomas, T. L. (2004, August). Improve your writing by outlining concepts more effectively. *Inside Microsoft Word, 11*(8), 8–10.

CHAPTER 4

Researching Your Outline

Chapter Learning Objectives:

- Define annotation and its origins.
- Explain the advantages of annotation.
- Explain and discuss the purpose of an annotated outline.
- Explain the annotated bibliography process.
- Identify and discuss the tools for annotation.
- Summarize the benefits of a modified annotated outline/bibliography.

Annotation

WHAT IS ANNOTATION?

Annotations are used to assist with understanding a text by writing notes, comments, or source/reference information about an article or book. The concept is not new. It actually is derived from the word *exegesis*, which is a critical understanding, interpretation, and explanation of text. Exegesis is derived from the Greek word *exegeisthai*, which means to explain. Other synonyms for exegesis are paraphrasing, clarification, summarizing, or interpretation (Capella University Writing Center, 2007; Liu, 2006; Merriam-Webster, 2017).

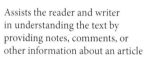

annotation

Assists the reader and writer in understanding the text by providing notes, comments, or other information about an article or book.

exegesis

A critical understanding, interpretation, and explanation of a text. Comes from the Greek *exegeisthai*, "to explain."

TYPES OF ANNOTATIONS

Types of annotations can vary. Generally, annotations comprise:

- Topic sentences
- Comments, notes, or explanations

- Sources or reference information
- Descriptive information about each source

ADVANTAGES OF ANNOTATING

Experienced writers will naturally annotate. As a student writer, annotating should become a habit. Creating this habit has several benefits:

- Assists in processing new information and acquiring new skills
- Increases the ability to handle new learning assignments
- Improves learning behaviors to produce positive writing results
- Allows for comprehension, not recall
- Produces better critical and analytical writing

WHEN TO ANNOTATE

First, annotate text that needs further comprehension or understanding. Second, annotate assignments where scholarly evidence is needed to support your argument. Finally, annotate when important facts need to be committed to memory.

HOW TO ANNOTATE

When annotating text, you can underline, circle, or highlight words or passages; use question marks; or obtain definitions of words to understand text. Writing in the margins allows for comments, paraphrasing, or clarification, retention, and reflection of attitude toward the text you are reading (Diyanni, 2002). Summarize important ideas; add examples to provide evidence and support the text. It is a good idea to define new words or mark confusing passages so you can gain insight from the instructor or revisit at a later date. Remember, annotation is a process to gain understanding.

annotated outline

Adds citation information and provides evidentiary support for each section and topic of an outline.

FIGURE 4.1

Basic Outline

I.   Charismatic Leadership

    A.   Social Proximity and Identity

    B.   Ethics

Annotated Outline

After creating your outline, you must locate research to support your topics. The **annotated outline** is an extremely useful tool for integrating this research into your project. An annotated outline adds citation information and provides evidentiary support for each section and topic. It is also an effective tool for organizing your research. When writing your annotated outline, ask your instructor about the format. There are three distinctive approaches (Capella Writing Center, 2007; Morgan, 2016). Begin with a fully developed outline (Figure 4.1).

The first type of annotated outline is adding citation or source information under each topic (Figure 4.2).

I.   Charismatic Leadership

      Paulsen, N., Maldonado, D., Callan, C., & Ayoko, O. (2009). Charismatic leadership
          change and innovation in an R&D organization. *Journal of Organizational Change
          Management, 22(5)*, 511-523. doi.org/10.1108/09534810910983479.

      A. Social Proximity and Identity
          Conger, J. A., & Kanungo, R. N. (1987). Toward a Behavioral Theory of
              Charismatic Leadership in Organizational Settings. *Academy of Management
              Review, 12(4)*, 637–647. doi.org/10.5465/AMR.1987.4306715.

      B. Ethics
          Howell, J. M., & Avolio, B. J. (1992). The ethics of charismatic leadership:
              submission or liberation? *The Executive, 6(2)*, 43–54.
              doi.org/10.5465/AME.1992.4274395.

FIGURE 4.2

Annotated Outline

The second type of annotated outline is to add the citation, then provide descriptive information about the citation (Figure 4.3).

I.   Charismatic Leadership
      Paulsen, N., Maldonado, D., Callan, C., & Ayoko, O. (2009). Charismatic leadership,
          change, and innovation in an R&D organization. *Journal of Organizational
          Change Management, 22*(5), 511–523. doi: 10.1108/09534810910983479

          The purpose of this paper is to investigate the effects of the charismatic di-
          mension of transformational leadership on team processes and innovative
          outcomes in research and development teams.

      A. Social Proximity and Identity
          Conger, J. A., & Kanungo, R. N. (1987). Toward a behavioral theory of char-
              ismatic leadership in organizational settings. *Academy of Manage-
              ment Review, 12*(4), 637–647. doi: 10.5465/AMR.1987.4306715

          Conger and Kanungo attempt to create a conceptual framework that opera-
          tionalizes the concept of charismatic leadership and to identify the compo-
          nents that would assist in creating the framework.

      B. Ethics
          Howell, J. M., & Avolio, B. J. (1992). The ethics of charismatic leadership:
              submission or liberation? *The Executive, 6*(2), 43–54. doi: 10.5465/
              AME.1992.4274395

          Howell and Avolio (1992) examined the impact that ethical and unethical
          charismatic leaders have on followers' behavior and how organizations can
          develop ethical charismatic leaders.

FIGURE 4.3

*Annotated Outline with
Descriptive Information*

The third way to add annotations to your outline is to add the citation and a topic sentence (Figure 4.4).

I. Charismatic Leadership
    Paulsen, N., Maldonado, D., Callan, C., & Ayoko, O. (2009). Charismatic leadership, change, and innovation in an R&D organization. *Journal of Organizational Change Management, 22*(5), 511–523. doi: 10.1108/09534810910983479

    Charisma is viewed as an essential leadership quality that provides a path to organizational transformation. Leaders who adopt a charismatic leadership style teem with confidence, vision, and purpose.

A. Social Proximity and Identity
    Conger, J. A., & Kanungo, R. N. (1987). Toward a behavioral theory of charismatic leadership in organizational settings. *Academy of Management Review, 12*(4), 637–647. doi: 10.5465/AMR.1987.4306715

    The theory of charismatic leadership describes leaders' behaviors in organizations. This theory focuses on a certain set of leaders' behaviors that can be directly observed from the follower's perspective. Charismatic leadership may be described as one-role leaders' display at work.

B. Ethics
    Howell, J. M., & Avolio, B. J. (1992). The ethics of charismatic leadership: submission or liberation? *The Executive, 6*(2), 43–54. doi: 10.5465/AME.1992.4274395

    The term charisma does not distinguish between good or evil, moral or immoral. This is the risk when a leader is termed charismatic. The study found that there are seven key behaviors of charismatic leadership: (1) exercising power, (2) creating vision, (3) communicating with followers, (4) accepting feedback, (5) stimulating followers intellectually, (6) developing followers, and (7) instituting moral standards.

By creating an annotated outline, it provides visual evidence of research conducted and helps determine whether more research is needed to fulfill the requirements of the assignment.

Annotated Bibliography

annotated bibliography

Gives written information about the content of each reference. The summary serves as the citation information, not the citation itself.

An **annotated bibliography** lists your citations, each of which is followed by a summary of content. It informs the reader of the currency, authority, accuracy, accessibility, relevancy, and purpose of the chosen citation or reference. The annotated bibliography moves the project from the research phase to the drafting phase of the writing process. Annotations can be a minimum of 150 words to several paragraphs long (Capella University Writing Center, 2008; Engle, 2017).

Writing an annotated bibliography is not about the outline. The outline is still important, but annotated bibliographies take the writer into the drafting stage of the writing process. Depending on the category of annotated bibliography, developing content is much easier because it is the research that gives you the words and ideas for writing one source at a time. Figure 4.5 illustrates the annotated bibliography process.

ANNOTATED BIBLIOGRAPHY PROCESS

1. Locate scholarly journals, articles, books, periodicals, or documents that contain information that can be applied to your topic.
2. Cite chosen documents in the appropriate writing style (APA, MLA, or Chicago).
3. Alphabetize your citations. They can also be organized by chronology, theme, or some other aspect of a topic.
4. Write annotations underneath each source.

FIGURE 4.5

Annotated Bibliography Process

Categories of Annotations

Summaries can be descriptive, summative, or evaluative.

DESCRIPTIVE ANNOTATED BIBLIOGRAPHY

A **descriptive, or indicative, annotated bibliography** seeks to describe the actual reference or source. It incorporates the content of the article or book, and the author's conclusion. The question descriptive annotations answer is, "How does this source cover or address the topic of research?" They should not summarize the argument (Figure 4.6).

descriptive annotated bibliography

Seeks to describe the actual reference or source.

FIGURE 4.6

Descriptive Annotated Bibliography Example

> Makino, S., Chan, C., Isobe, T., & Beamish, P. (2007). Intended and unintended termination of international joint ventures. *Strategic Management Journal, 28*(11), 1113–1132. Retrieved from Business Source Complete database.
>
> The authors saw two major limitations within their work: first, the focus only on international joint ventures, because there are other forms of market entry, and second, the methodology. According to Makino, Isobe, and Beamish (2007), the observed association between the initial purposes of international joint-venture formation and longevity may be plausible but false. Future research should examine the extent to which previous intended and unintended termination decisions are formed. In addition, the future researcher could investigate the way in which firms learn from previous unintended international joint-venture terminations to increase the chances of a successful joint venture in the future.

SUMMATIVE ANNOTATED BIBLIOGRAPHY

Summative annotated bibliography

Summarizes the content, message, or argument of the annotated bibliography.

A **summative, or informative, annotated bibliography** summarizes the content, message, or argument of the citations. It can contain many elements, such as the main points, hypothesis, research questions, methodology, results, purpose, and conclusion. No evaluative comments are made when writing a summative annotated bibliography. It "provides the reader with a solid sense of the content of the article" (Capella University Writing Centre, 2008, p. 3). Writers might ask, "What is the difference between this and the abstract?" The summative annotated bibliography has more content than an abstract. An abstract is a summary of the entire paper that ranges between 150 and 250 words. Consider it as the main points of a research article. The abstract includes the findings of a research article, which are presented after the title page. The summative annotated bibliography summarizes each research source, not the entire paper (Figure 4.7).

FIGURE 4.7

Summative Annotated Bibliography Example

Slovic, P., Fischhoff, B., & Lichtenstein, S. (1977). Behavioral decision theory. *Annual Review of Psychology*, 281.

There are two facets to behavioral decision theory: normative and descriptive. Normative theory is concerned with prescribing a course of action that conforms mostly to the decision makers' beliefs, values, and culture. The crux of any nonprofit organization is a belief and value on how to help humanity. The decision to create a nonprofit is a value judgment. How these beliefs are incorporated into everyday decision making is where the descriptive theory comes into play. Descriptive theory describes a decision, which is incorporated into the beliefs and values of the decision maker. Nonprofit management displays traits of normative and descriptive theories because there is a constant struggle to implement business decisions while maintaining the values and beliefs of the organization.

Remember that a summative annotation does the following:

- Introduces the author and their qualifications
- Overviews the content of the article
- Contains purpose, methodology, results, and conclusion

EVALUATIVE ANNOTATED BIBLIOGRAPHY

evaluative annotated bibliography

Includes both descriptive and summative annotations with the addition of a crucial assessment of the article or book.

An **evaluative, or critical, annotated bibliography** includes both descriptive and summative annotations with the addition of a crucial assessment of the article or book. A critical assessment is an evaluation of the argumentative position and its overall usefulness. This usually includes a review of the data-collection method, results, or overall methodology as a part of the evaluation. The easiest way to write an evaluative annotated bibliography is to write as if you are writing the final paper. Essentially, you are in drafting mode because you are writing the paper source by source (Figure 4.8).

FIGURE 4.8

Evaluative Annotated Bibliography Example

Joshi, A., Lazarova, M. B., & Liao, H. (2009). Getting everyone on board: The role of inspirational leadership in geographically dispersed teams. *Organization Science, 20*(1), 240–252.

This research is based on the assumption that leaders are able to influence followers based on close relationships and personal contact. Leaders who engage in socialized relationships are able to provide followers with a "clear set of values and a means of expressing these values within the framework of collective action" (Howell & Shamir, 2005, p. 98). The purpose of this article is to analyze whether attitudes surveyed at the team level translate to overall improved team performance. Taking on social identity theory, researchers have suggested that leaders who display inspirational behaviors can build lasting connections between an individual's self-concept and a social group, thereby enhancing recognition with the social group. Because of their emphasis on building socialized relationships, these leaders attract attention to the team's mission, shared values, goals, objectives, ideology, and the interrelationships between followers' individual interests and team interests (Shamir et al., 1993). Thus, inspirational leaders can provide team members with a set of circumstances to applaud team accomplishments and other team members' assistance and build a broad basis for identification with the team. Based on teachings from situational theories of leadership and by constructing socialized relationships with followers, inspirational leaders can change the course of attention to a common vision for the team and encourage team members to go above and beyond subgroup disparity. In the absence of contiguity, inspirational leaders may potentially become the spokesperson for the group (Howell & Shamir, 2005; Kark & Shamir, 2002). A web survey was sent to 700 service employees working in geographically dispersed teams in a single multinational Fortune 500 hardware and software company. These employees were organized into 91 teams, and each team reported to a formally assigned leader.

After two rounds of reminder emails, 247 individuals responded to the surveys, resulting in a response rate of 35 percent. Respondents had an average of five years of organizational tenure and two years of tenure with the team. Of the sample, 73 percent were male, and 63 percent are located within the United States. The results support the argument that by fostering socialized relationships with team members, which rely on a shared message and emphasize the mission and goals of the team, inspirational leaders are able to foster attitudes directed at the collective team entity. Overall, the results suggest that inspirational leaders are important in all contexts but are more important in a highly volatile environment.

In summary, when you are writing your annotated bibliography, you will have a mixture of mainly summative and evaluative annotations. By placing these annotations in alphabetical order, the annotated bibliography will take shape (Figure 4.9).

FIGURE 4.9

Different Types of Annotated Bibliographies

Descriptive	Summative	Evaluative
• Main purpose of the article or book • Content of the article or book • Conclusion of the article • Theory used • Who is the audience? • 150 words to one or two paragraphs	• Introduces author and qualifications • Provides reader a summary of message, content, or argument • Contains hypothesis, methodology, data-collection procedure, results, and conclusion • Provides evaluative or judgmental comments • Increases length of annotation to several paragraphs	• Assesses the purpose and value of the article or book • States why the article is of interest • Identifies main point of article • Introduces key terms of central argument • Offers insight into a potential application • Addresses strengths and weaknesses of article or book • Identifies contribution to the literature of the subject • Supplies overall reaction to the article or book

Modified Annotated Outline/Bibliography

modified annotated outline/bibliography

Combines the outline, annotated outline, and annotated bibliography so the student views how the entire paper is assembled.

Modified annotated outlines/bibliographies (MAOBs) are designed to allow students to understand the real purpose of the writing process—the complete picture. The annotated outline allows for research on each topic, and the annotated bibliography dictates the description, summary, and analysis for each source you chose in your annotated outline. The MAOB combines the outline, annotated outline, and annotated bibliography so the student views how the entire paper is assembled. Once the MAOB combination occurs, it is quite easy to complete your assignment, document, or project (Figure 4.10).

FIGURE 4.10

I.   **Theory behind Capital Campaigns**
Lindahl, W. (2010). *Principles of fundraising: theory and practice.* Sudbury, MA: Jones and Bartlett Publishers.

According to Lindhal (2010), fundraising theory has developed from many different fields of management: marketing, psychology, organizational behavior, and sociology. Grants Economics accepts many different types of motivations, such as altruism, love, fear, malevolence, and self-interest for funding. The word "grant" in Grants Economics implies the process of giving or receiving foundation grants. The donor, recipient, or third party is sovereign in the grant's economy. Humanity, benevolence, and love are a part of an integrative subsystem of the grant economy. Under this type of economy, dependency is a potential weakness where the nonprofit is dependent on the donor for a long-term basis.

A.   **Capital Campaign and Fundraising Theory**
Andreoni, J. (1998). Toward a theory of charitable fund-raising. *Journal of Political Economy, 106*(6), 1186–1213.

The capital-theory model states that individuals are endowed with money that they allocate between buying private goods and gifts to the public. Capital campaigns are generally the origins of charitable nonprofit organizations. Many people have the misconception that a nonprofit is a free-riding institution. Capital campaigns heavily rely on seed grants and large leadership gifts that are publicly announced before the general fundraising drive begins. According to Andreoni (1998), "the rule of thumb for capital campaigns is that one-third of the goal must be raised in a 'quiet phase' before the public fund drive is launched" (p. 1187).

B.   **Social Exchange**
Becker, G. S. (1974). A theory of social interactions. *Journal of Political Economy, 82*(6), 1063–1093.

The theory of social interaction is based on the social exchange theory. A person earns a certain dollar amount of income. This income is the sum of the individual's monetary income plus the value of his or her social environment and is reflected in the characteristics of other people that affect the individual.

C.   **Warm-Glow Giving Theory**
Andreoni, J. (1990). Impure altruism and donations to public goods: A theory of warm-glow giving. *Economic Journal, 100*(401), 464–477.

There are many factors that influence a person's decision to make a donation. Andreoni (1990) believed that people are motivated by a desire to win prestige, respect, friendships, or other social and psychological objectives. Motives for giving are not all altruistic. "Clearly social pressure, guilt, sympathy, or simply a desire for a 'warm glow' may play an important role in decision of agents" (p. 464). A key understanding in the warm-glow model is basic motivation. Is the donor made happy because others are helped, or is the donor made happy by giving to a good cause? The egoist does not care how many people are helped; a donation was made because it felt right and now it feels good. The warm-glow giving theory provides support that potential donors gain satisfaction from the act of donation to a public service organization.

In summary, using the modified annotated outline/bibliography allows the writer to be guided by the outline while writing underneath each source. Once complete, the following occurs:

1. The outline becomes headings in your paper.
2. The sources become your reference page.
3. The text from the annotated bibliography becomes the content within your writing project. Using a MAOB is a helpful tool for integrating annotations into a working writing draft.

Tools for Annotation

MICROSOFT WORD

Microsoft Word makes annotation easy through the use of the Comment feature. Using the Comment feature, you can insert, reply to, change, show, hide, or delete comments in a box that will appear in the margins of a document. To begin using the Comment feature:

1. Select **Review** on the menu.
2. Select the text or block of text on which you would like to comment.
3. Click on **New Comment** (Figures 4.11 and 4.11.1).

FIGURE 4.11

How to Use Comments in Microsoft Word

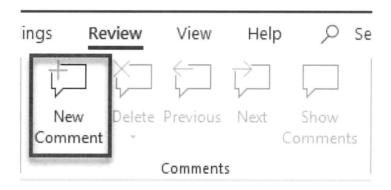

FIGURE 4.11.1

How to Use Comments in Microsoft Word, Con.

When annotating text, you can underline, circle, highlight words or passages, use question marks, or obtain definitions of words to understand text. Writing in the margins allows for comments, paraphrasing, or clarification, retention, and reflection of attitude towards the text being read (Diyanni, 2002). Summarize important ideas, add examples to give evidence and support of the text. It is a good idea to define unfamiliar words, mark passages that are confusing to revisit at a later date or mark passages so you can gain insight from the instructor. Remember, annotation is process to gain understanding.

Cassandra Baker 2 minutes ago
This is an example of using annotations in Microsoft word.
Reply   Resolve

Using comments is a great way to communicate with other team members and give feedback on a document. Also, you can reply to a comment within a document that has been emailed to you. The Resolve feature allows the user to close out any comments that are no longer useful without deleting the comment. If you change your mind and would like to reopen the comment, then the word "Resolve" changes to the word "Reopen" (Microsoft Corporation, 2017; Lambert & Cox, 2013).

MICROSOFT POWERPOINT

Annotations are easy to write in Microsoft PowerPoint because you can add notes, insert comments, and add text boxes and caption boxes. Also, there is a new feature called Ink Annotation (see Figure 4.12 and 4.12.1).

FIGURE 4.12

How to Use Comments in PowerPoint

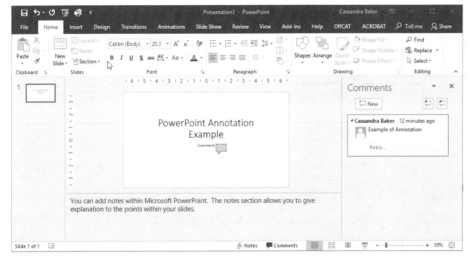

FIGURE 4.12.1

How to Use Comments in PowerPoint, Con.

OTHER NOTABLE MENTIONS

Microsoft Office and Ink

Within Microsoft Office (Excel, Word, and PowerPoint), there is a feature called Ink. Ink allows you to annotate on your smartphone, pad, or other touch devices. Using Ink, you can "make notes, highlight portions of your text, quickly create shapes, or write math equations and have them converted to text on touch devices or pen-enabled devices" (Microsoft Corporation, 2016, para. 2) (Figure 4.13).

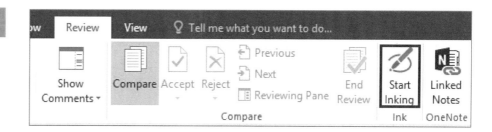

Adobe DC

Files that are saved in a Portable Document Format (PDF) can be easily annotated. Adobe DC has a drawing markup toolbar that allows for comments, highlighting, sticky notes, underlining, and strikethrough. According to Adobe Systems Incorporated (2017), "The commenting tools are made available in the secondary toolbar of the Comment feature. Comments are notes and drawings that communicate ideas or provide feedback for PDFs" (para. 1). Additionally, the annotation bar on the comment bar has a search feature for locating multiple comments quickly (Figure 4.14).

Choose **Tools** then **Comment** to open the Comment toolbar. The comments you add to the document are displayed in the right pane.

FIGURE 4.14

Annotations and Drawing Markup Tools Overview

	A sticky note has a note icon that appears on the page and a pop-up note for your text message. Sticky notes can be added anywhere within your PDF. Sticky notes allow the user to add annotations.
	Highlights text. Text can be highlighted in different colors.
	Adds note to replace text.
	Inserts text at cursor.

T	Adds text anywhere within the PDF.	
[T]	Adds a text box.	
✎	Draws free form.	
◇	Erases.	

Google Keep

Google Keep (www.google.com/keep) is a website tool that allows the user to save and annotate websites and add labels. Moreover, there is a collaboration feature to share websites and notes with other people. Google Keep is a Chrome extension with note-taking abilities that integrates with Google Docs. The Google Keep browser extension can be downloaded from the Chrome Web Store.

Summary

In chapter 3, we discussed the real purpose of an outline. Chapter 4 takes that outline into the discovery phase of writing and details the annotation of an outline through research. Researching an outline allows the writer to begin the drafting stage by making notes, sentences, citations, and descriptions for each topic on their outline. Creating an annotated outline or annotated bibliography allows the writer to validate the research available for each topic of discussion. A modified annotated outline/bibliography allows the student to write, research, and organize without losing track of citations.

Key Terms

Annotated bibliography
Annotated outline
Annotation
Descriptive annotated bibliography

Evaluative annotated bibliography
Exegesis
Modified annotated outline/bibliography
Summative annotated bibliography

Review Questions

1. List and define the types of annotations used in writing.
2. List the advantages of annotating.
3. Define and explain the origins of annotating.
4. When is it appropriate to annotate?
5. List and describe the three types of annotated outlines.
6. Why are annotated outlines used in research?
7. At what stage of the writing process do annotated bibliographies begin?
8. Explain the annotated bibliography process.
9. Summarize the use of the modified annotated outline/bibliography.
10. List the tools used for annotation.

References

Adobe Systems Incorporated. (2017). *Use annotation and drawing markup tools to add comments in PDFs, Adobe Acrobat DC.* Retrieved from https://helpx.adobe.com/acrobat/using/commenting-pdfs.html

Capella University Writing Center. (2007, May). *Developing an annotated outline.* Retrieved from http://www.capella.edu/interactivemedia/onlinewritingcenter/downloads/handoutDevAnnotatedOutline.pdf

Capella University Writing Center. (2008, September). *Annotated bibliographies—Capella University.* Retrieved from http://www.capella.edu/interactivemedia/onlineWritingCenter/downloads/annotatedBibliography.pdf

DiYanni, R. J. (2002). *One Hundred Great Essays.* Boston, MA: Pearson.

Engle, M. (2017, March 17). *LibGuides: How to prepare an annotated bibliography: The annotated bibliography.* Retrieved from http://guides.library.cornell.edu/c.php?g=32342&p=203789

Lambert, J., & Cox, J. (2013). *Microsoft Word 2013 Step by Step* (1st ed.). Redmond, WA: Microsoft Press.

Liu, K. (2006). Annotation as an index to critical writing. *Urban Education, 41*(2), 192–207. Retrieved from https://doi.org/10.1177/0042085905282261

Merriam-Webster. (2017). *Definition of EXEGESIS.* Retrieved from https://www.merriam-webster.com/dictionary/exegesis

Microsoft Corporation. (2016). *Draw and write with ink in Office 2016—Office Support.* Retrieved from https://support.office.com/en-us/article/Draw-and-write-with-ink-in-Office-2016-c00b7319-2b50-4784-8114-47593d991c5c

Microsoft Corporation. (2017). *Insert or delete a comment—Word.* Retrieved from https://support.office.com/en-us/article/Insert-or-delete-a-comment-8D3F868A-867E-4DF2-8C68-BF96671641E2

Morgan, L. L. (2016). *Library guides: How to prepare an annotated bibliography: Annotated bibliography.* Retrieved from http://libguides.library.nd.edu/annotated-bibliography/overview

CHAPTER 5

Internet Research

Chapter Learning Objectives:

- Identify and discuss the bibliographic trail and its importance in locating scholarly research sources.
- Explain temporal citations in Internet research using Google Scholar.
- Discuss the advantages and disadvantages of using Wikipedia.
- Discuss Boolean operators in Internet searching.
- Discuss how file types are used as limiters in Internet searching.
- Compare and contrast Google Special Syntax with Bing Query Language.

Temporal Citations

temporal citation

Bibliographic information that moves forward or backward in time.

FOLLOWING THE BIBLIOGRAPHIC TRAIL: RETROSPECTIVE

Many students sit at a computer to begin researching, not having a clue where to start. They look at the computer monitor as if it were a giant black hole. The first place to begin your research is by utilizing the course textbook. When reading the textbook, you will not be reading for content, but for **references** about your topic. For example, if you are taking an organizational behavior class and you must write a paper on older workers . . .

references

A list of books, magazines, scholarly work, or websites that serves as evidence to support research topic. Also known as a bibliography or sources.

1. The first step would be reading the section of the textbook on older workers (see Figure 5.1).
2. Next, find the references. Many textbooks are written according to *The Chicago Manual of Style*. Other textbooks are written in APA or MLA. The in-text citations in Figure 5.1 are written in *The Chicago Manual of Style*.

3. Depending upon the writing, the in-text citations will appear differently. For example, in Figure 5.1, you see a subscripted number nine and ten. Those are in-text citations identifying the source used to write that section of the text.
4. To find the reference, look at the back of the chapter or back of the book. If the references are at the back of the book, they are usually listed by chapter.
5. Search for the number found for the in-text citation on older workers and you will find your reference used to write that paragraph.

bibliographic trail

A retrospective review at the bibliography or reference page of a journal article or book. Used to locate and follow research.

bibliography

A list of books, magazines, scholarly works, or websites that serves as evidence to support research topic. Also known as references or sources.

Once you have located the references, then you can search for that article or book within your college or university library databases. Remember, those references are there for your use. By following the bibliographic trail, you will cut your research time in half. You are now squeezing the juice out of the textbook. Following the bibliographic trail is the start of locating articles, journals, books, or periodicals to complete your annotated outline or bibliography.

FIGURE 5.1

Following the Bibliographic Trail in a Textbook

Employers express mixed feelings about the older worker. They see a number of positive qualities older workers bring to their jobs, such as experience, judgment, a strong work ethic, and commitment to quality. But older workers are also perceived as lacking flexibility and resisting new technology. And when organizations are actively seeking individuals who are adaptable and open to change, the negatives associated with age clearly hinder the initial hiring of older workers and increase the likelihood they will be let go during cutbacks.

In-text citation written in Chicago Style.

Now let's take a look at the evidence. What effect does age actually have on turnover, absenteeism, productivity, and satisfaction? The older you get, the less likely you are to quit your job. That conclusion is based on studies of the age–turnover relationship. Of course, this shouldn't be too surprising. As workers get older, they have fewer alternative job opportunities as their skills have become more specialized to certain types of work. Their long tenure also tends to provide them with higher wage rates, longer paid vacations, and more attractive pension benefits.

Reference Page. Also known as Work Cited, End Notes, or Bibliography.

9. K. A. Wrenn and T. J. Maurer, "Beliefs About Older Workers' Learning and Development Behavior in Relation to Beliefs About Malleability of Skills, Age-Related Decline, and Control," *Journal of Applied Social Psychology* 34, no. 2 (2004), pp. 223–242; and R. A. Posthuma and M. A. Campion, "Age Stereotypes in the Workplace: Common Stereotypes, Moderators, and Future Research Directions," *Journal of Management* 35 (2009), pp. 158–188.
10. T. W. H. Ng and D. C. Feldman, "Re-examining the Relationship Between Age and Voluntary Turnover," *Journal of Vocational Behavior* 74 (2009), pp. 283–294.

Note: Excerpt from *Organizational Behavior*, 16th edition by Stephen P. Robbins and Timothy A. Judge, Published by Prentice Hall. Copyright © 2015 by Pearson Education, Inc.

Another example of following the bibliographic trail is using the actual article. Figure 5.2 is an article from the *Journal of Marketing Management*. From the excerpt in the journal, the reader can follow the bibliographic trail using the reference page of the article.

Based on Methlie and Gressgard (2006), four key structural conditions are considered. Market conditions relate to the structure of the optimum channel network, size of market, industry growth, competition (relating to number of vendors and distribution partners in the channel), long-term strategic trends and the frequency of mergers and acquisitions. Product conditions relate to technology. Here there is a constant evolution of new products and technology, products superseding other products and short product life-cycles.

Medicines Australia (2007). Australian pharmaceutical industry at a crossroad. *Medicines Australia member economic survey.*

Methlie, L. B., & Gressgard, L. J. (2006). Exploring the relationship between structural market conditions and business conduct in mobile data service markets. *Journal of Electronic Research, 7*(1), 14–26.

Miles, M. B., & Huberman, A. M. (1994). *Qualitative data analysis: An expanded sourcebook.* Newbury Park, CA: Sage.

Morgan, R. M., & Hunt, S. D. (1994). The commitment–trust theory of relationship marketing. *Journal of Marketing, 58,* 20–38 (July).

Adapted from "How channels evolve: A historical explanation" by N. Bairstow and L. Young, *Industrial Marketing Management, 41*(3), p. 385–393. Copyright 2012 by Elsevier Inc.

FIGURE 5.2

Following the Bibliographic Trail in an Article

Following the bibliographic trail is also known as backward citation. Often when following the bibliographic trail, you can locate seminal work. Seminal work is landmark original research of importance. Most landmark research is frequently cited in other journals, books, articles, and trade magazines.

seminal work

Landmark original research. Seminal comes from the word semen, which mean seed. Also called germinal work.

CITATION INDEXING: PROSPECTIVE

Citations were created to help retrieve information. They are references or sources linked to a published work such as a book, journal article, or magazine. Usually, the bibliographic trail is moving backward in time to find sources that support a writer's claim. However, a technique called citation indexing allows the user to move forward in time. The researcher views which later documents were cited in earlier documents. This allows the user to evaluate an article or source's credibility, reputation, impact, and popularity (Booth, Colomb, Williams, Bizup, & Fitzgerald, 2016). For example, imagine you are writing a paper on the topic of authentic leadership. Place the search term "authentic leadership" in a database such as Google Scholar.

citations

Also known as references or sources, linked to published works such as books, journal articles, or magazines.

Google Scholar (scholar.google.com) then gives you a list of results. Locating the words "Cited by" will allow you to move forward. As you can see from Figure 5.3, Google Scholar allows the user to move forward in time by locating other scholars who have used the referenced article in their work. Following the citation trails allows the writer to find newer articles based on an original document that is closely related to their topic.

sources

A list of books, magazines, scholarly works, or websites. Also known as bibliography or references.

citation indexing

The researcher views which later documents were cited in earlier documents.

FIGURE 5.3

Citation Indexing: Prospective

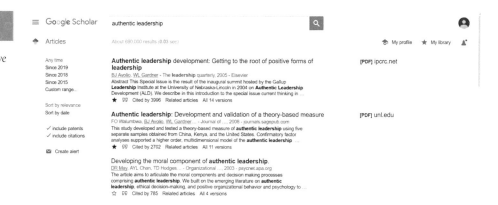

Citation indexing allows for article linking and trend tracking. Cite Seer is a scholarly digital library (citeseerx.ist.psu.edu/index) that allows for citation indexing. A researcher can find many free articles from this site (Figure 5.4).

FIGURE 5.4

Cite Seer Citation Indexing

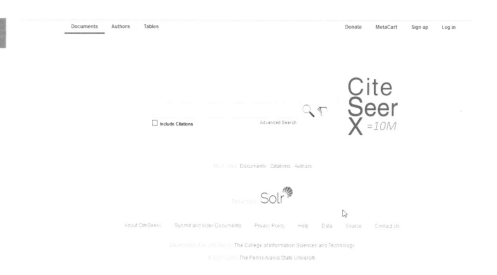

Citation indexes can be used to:

1. Find other publications of interest
2. Determine the importance of the publication
3. Determine the popularity of the publication
4. Locate new and emerging areas of study

The Wikipedia Trail

Wikipedia

Open-source encyclopedia that is collaboratively edited online.

Wikipedia is a free online open-access encyclopedia where content can be modified by anyone who has access to the Internet and creates a username and password with Wikipedia. Academics around the world distrust Wikipedia because it does not meet the quality standard of the academic community and it challenges the traditional mode of knowledge distribution (Jemielniak & Aibar, 2016). The academic community is concerned that Wikipedia lacks **accuracy** and completeness. Using collaborative community for modifying content has replaced the traditional editing controls and peer reviews (Azzam et al., 2017; Kousha & Thelwall, 2017).

accuracy

Reliability and validity of information.

Although accuracy, reliability, and completeness are the concerns of college instructors, it is not the concern of the average student. Huang, Shi, Chen, and Chow (2016) acknowledge that information accuracy, **validity**, and trustworthiness are not why students use Wikipedia, so there must be a compromise made between student and instructor.

validity

Information was collected using sound research methods and was correctly cited when published.

Use Wikipedia as a starting point for learning available information and resources on a topic (Okoli, Mehdi, Mesgari, Nielsen, & Lanamäki, 2014). By reviewing scholarly articles within Wikipedia, students can clearly identify then locate the information using a college library database, allowing them to distinguish fabricated information.

Do not cite Wikipedia as a source; however, use it to mine the bibliographic information for scholarly sources or books housed within a college library. In other words, use Wikipedia for citation extraction, not for scholarly content. The steps below are instructions to follow the Wikipedia trail:

1. Locate topic in Wikipedia.
2. Read the content to gain understanding of the topic.
3. Locate references section at the bottom of the web page.
4. Locate articles published by scholarly journals or books.
5. Using your college library databases, look up the article by title or journal title.

Now, you are using Wikipedia in your research, but you are not citing Wikipedia as a scholarly source. This is a happy compromise between student and instructor.

Internet Searching

The internet is a wonderful invention that allows users to have instantaneous information about any topic. When students receive a research assignment, the first place before going to the college library is to check the internet. Various websites will create a sea of search results that ranks in the millions, and students can become lost. Most students click page one, then page two, and that is when the frustration begins. You may say, "I can't find anything!" To alleviate this frustration, Google and Bing have something called special **syntax**, advanced operators, or advanced query language that lets users search for specific types of information. Basically, these advanced operators narrow search results, allowing you to search with precision.

syntax

A formation or group of words allowing formalized search and access to information on the Internet.

Boolean Operators

Boolean searching

Also called Boolean logic or Boolean operators. Consists of the conjunction words AND, OR, and NOT used in Internet and database searching.

Boolean Operators, also called Boolean Logic, are simple words (AND, OR, NOT) used as conjunctions to define a logical relationship when using keyword search terms. In other words, **Boolean searches** allow you to combine words and phrases to increase or limit your search. Using Boolean Operators results in a time-saving, focused, and productive search. They can create a restricted search, reducing the amount of record results, or an expanded search, broadening the amount of record results returned (Cathey, 2008).

Flexible Inclusion

OR

flexible inclusion

Using different search syntaxes to expand search results.

Flexible inclusion allows for the expansion of search results. The OR operator combines terms that are synonymous. This operator is misunderstood because it is not one or the other, which is a type of exclusion. Actually, the OR operator means more than one. Another meaning is "at least one is required" (boolean-blackbelt.com). The results of your search will contain at least one of your keyword search terms.

> Example: leader OR principal

> Example: oppression OR persecution

OR will yield many results, so it can be confusing to use. It is best to mix this operator with other search operators or commands to narrow your results.

NESTING

nesting

Term for allowing for an Internet search to be performed in word order. Uses parentheses to include synonyms or alternate terms that may describe your topic.

Nesting allows an Internet search to be performed in word order. You use parentheses to include synonyms or alternate terms that may describe your topic. By using nesting, you can combine the operators AND plus OR in a single statement (Athabasca University, 2017). The following are examples of using nests in an Internet search:

> Example: (hate crimes (blacks OR African Americans))

> Example: (obesity AND (adolescent OR teenagers))

The results will include the sequence of the search term.

Addition and Inclusion

AND

The word AND means to combine keywords to include a search term in the results. It can also combine keywords to narrow the search results. When using the AND command, you are now searching for two words in your search results.

FIGURE 5.5

Addition and Inclusion

+

The plus symbol is the same as the AND command, and it can be used in its place. Addition and inclusion commands of AND/+ are indication and intersection of a relationship between two search terms (Figure 5.5).

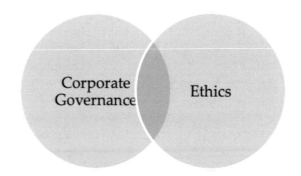

Your search term would be written as

      Example 1: (corporate governance) AND ethics

      Example 2: corporate governance AND ethics

Both search terms will yield the same results.

Negation and Exclusion

NOT

The NOT operator is an exclusive command that indicates not including a keyword in your search term. However, when searching in Google, it is easier to use the minus (−) sign in place of NOT.

The minus sign is the same as the NOT operator in that it excludes specific search terms from your query.

      Example 1: (corporate governance) AND ethics − books

      Example 2: corporate governance AND ethics − books

The above examples search the Internet for "corporate governance" including the word "ethics," but eliminating all "books."

Phrase Searching

phrase searching

Involves using quotation marks around two or more keywords.

Phrase searching involves using quotation marks around two or more keywords. By doing this, the search engine is no longer looking for two separate words; now, the words become one phrase.

For example, if you place the words *gun control* in your search-engine query box, you are searching for two words: gun then control. When you place quotation marks around the search phrase "gun control," now it is one phrase, not two separate keywords.

Use quotations around keyword search terms when:

1. Looking up proper names
2. Searching for plagiarism
3. Locating recommendations

Quotations are a social operand that mix well with other Google syntaxes. Phrase searching narrows your search for more accurate results.

Wild Cards

wild card

Also called truncation. A search syntax that is supported by the asterisk (*) symbol. Each asterisk represents a word replacement or placeholder for the remainder of the phrase.

Wild cards, also called truncation, are supported by the asterisk (*) symbol. Each asterisk represents a word replacement or placeholder for the remainder of the phrase.

> Example: ten schools of * Mintzberg

The results of this example will yield information on the ten schools of thought on strategy formation by Henry Mintzberg. Using wildcards is a useful search technique when locating poetry, music lyrics, or famous quotations.

Google Search Syntax

Google syntaxes are search operators that sift through the millions of web pages, making web searching more precise (Dornfest, Bausch, & Calishain, 2006). Precise Internet searches use syntax. Syntax is a group of words allowing formalized search and access of information on the Internet. This is not a new form of searching. It has been used by programmers and librarians for many years. Once students use syntax searching, they find it is the only way to search the Internet because it saves time.

INTITLE

The intitle: syntax limits searches to the word or phrase in the title of the website. This syntax is a social syntax because it can be combined effectively with other syntaxes. A variation of this syntax is allintitle:, which does not always mix well with other syntaxes.

> Example: intitle:"gun control"

> Example: intitle:"charismatic leadership"

INTEXT

The intext: syntax limits searches to the body text of the website. This syntax is great for keywords or obscure phrases. Searching for common words using this syntax will increase your results. Additionally, this syntax ignores text in links, titles, and web addresses.

INURL

The inurl: syntax restricts a search to web addresses, better known as Universal Resource Locators (URL). Using this syntax allows the searcher to narrow a search to a website. This is a social syntax because it mixes well with other syntaxes.

For example, if you wanted to search the Small Business Administration (SBA) for a marketing plan, the syntax would be:

> Example: "marketing plan" inurl:www.sba.gov

> Example: intitle:"marketing plan" inurl:www.sba.gov

Another example is searching the Cable News Network (CNN) website for articles on gun control. The syntax would be:

> Example: "gun control" inurl:www.cnn.com

> Example: intitle:"gun control" inurl:www.cnn.com

SITE

Using this syntax allows you to restrict searches to top-level domain names or sites.

> Example: "medical marijuana" site:gov

> Example: intitle:"medical marijuana" site:gov

In this example, a search is conducted on the phrase "medical marijuana" within a United States government website. The search results will include federal, state, and local government sites. This is a good search for obtaining information about government material on a topic. Figure 5.6 shows the top-level domains that can be used with the inurl: syntax.

FIGURE 5.6

Top-Level Domains

.com	US Commercial Sites
.coop	Business Cooperatives
.edu	US Education Sites
.gov	US Government Sites
.info	US Information Sites
.mil	US Military Sites
.net	Internet Administrative Sites
.org	Organization Sites (Nonprofits)

INANCHOR

anchor

An anchor link is a web link that allows users to jump to a specific point on a website page.

The inanchor: operators allow a keyword search within the URL or web address link anchors. The **anchor** is the descriptive text of a web address. "An anchor link is a web link that allows users to jump to a specific point on a website page. It saves the need to scroll and skim read—and makes navigation easier" (Merry, 2017, para. 1). Finally, it is a useful syntax to limit search to pertinent sites.

Example: charismatic leadership inanchor:ethical

This example requires that all returned results be relevant to charismatic leadership and contain the word "ethical" in the anchors of linking pages.

LINK

The link: operator returns a list of web pages that are linked or pointed to a specific URL.

Example: link:www.amazon.com

The search operator link: is considered an antisocial syntax because it cannot be mixed with other search operators.

DATERANGE

The daterange: operator allows you to search the indexing date of a website, not the creation date. Basically, this syntax limits your search to a specific date range. Note that date ranges can change depending on how many times Google indexes a site. The daterange: syntax must be expressed with the Julian calendar date, not Gregorian.

To convert from the Gregorian to Julian calendar use the Julian Date Converter at the United States Naval Observatory website (aa.usno.navy.mil/data/docs/JulianDate.php).

Example: intitle:"medical marijuana" daterange:2452389-2452389
(April 24, 2002)

Example intitle:"medical marijuana" daterange:2457157.5-2457157.5
(May 15, 2015)

FILETYPE

The filetype: syntax searches file formats by allowing you to indicate a specific file extension. A **file format** is encoded information that is stored for a particular software application, and file extensions or suffixes specify the type of file. The Internet comprises files and databases. Figure 5.7 illustrates the most common file formats for use with filetype syntax. This operator is a sociable syntax because it mixes well with other syntax so you can search with precision.

> Example: "marketing plan" filetype:xls

The mixed syntax searches for the phrase "marketing plan" that only has Microsoft Excel file extensions.

> Example: intitle:"hate crimes" filetype:pdf site:gov

This is a mixed syntax to search government websites for the phrase "hate crimes" contained only in Portable Document Format (PDF) files.

file format

Encoded information that is stored for a particular software application.

FIGURE 5.7

Most Common File Formats

Word Processor File Format			Presentation File Format		
doc or docx	MS Word		odp	Open Office Presentation	
odt	Open Office		ppt	Microsoft PowerPoint Presentation	
pages	Apple iWork Pages Document		pps	PowerPoint Slide Show	
pdf	Portable Document Format		pez	Prezi	
rtf	Rich Text Format				
txt	Text Document				
wpd	Word Perfect				
Spreadsheet File Format			Video File Format		
ods	Open Office Spreadsheet		flv	Flash	
xls	Microsoft Excel		mp4 or mpeg4	Motion Picture Expert Group	
			mov	Apple QuickTime	
			rm	Real Media	
			wmv	Windows Media Player	
			vob	DVD File	
Audio File Format			Image File Format		
mp3	Compressed Audio File		bmp	Windows Bitmap	
midi	Musical Instrument Digital Interface		gif	Graphics Interchange	
wav	Windows Audio File		jpeg	Joint Photographic Experts Group	
wma	Windows Media Audio		png	Portable Network Graphic	
wpl	Windows Media Player Playlist		tif or tiff	Tagged Image File Format	

RELATED

The related: syntax allows you to search for websites that are similar. This is a good syntax to find competitor websites.

Example: related:www.ebscohost.com

EBSCO is a leading aggregator that houses databases, journal articles, and books. If you want to find other websites that are similar, you would use the above syntax (Figure 5.8).

Related Syntax Search Results Example

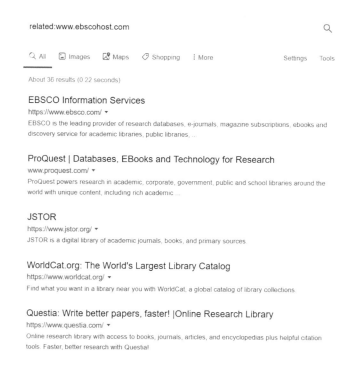

DEFINE

This search syntax allows you to define words using the Google search engine (Figure 5.9).

CALCULATOR

Now you can use a calculator over the Internet. Go to www.google.com. Once at the Google desktop, search the word "calculator" (Figure 5.10).

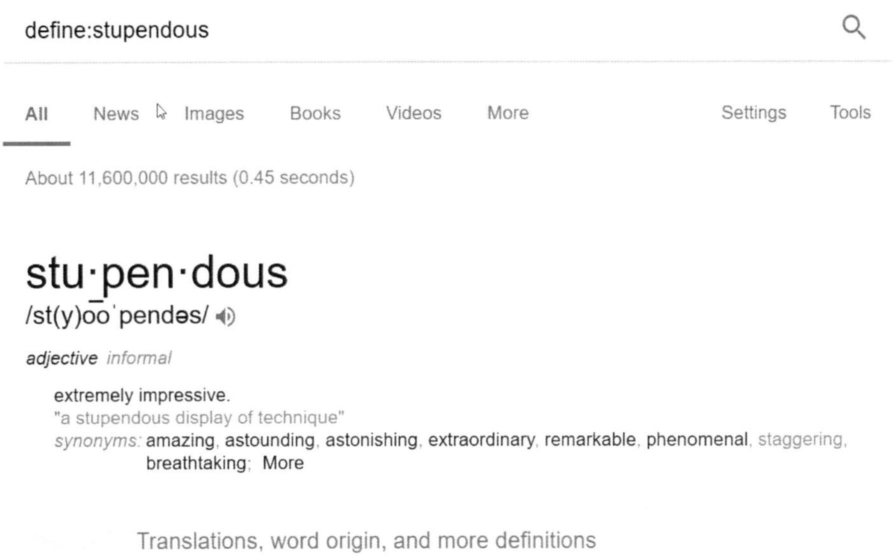

define:stupendous   🔍

All   News 🔖 Images   Books   Videos   More   Settings   Tools

About 11,600,000 results (0.45 seconds)

stu·pen·dous
/st(y)oo'pendəs/ 🔊

adjective *informal*

extremely impressive.
"a stupendous display of technique"
synonyms: amazing, astounding, astonishing, extraordinary, remarkable, phenomenal, staggering,
breathtaking; More

Translations, word origin, and more definitions

FIGURE 5.9

Define Syntax Example

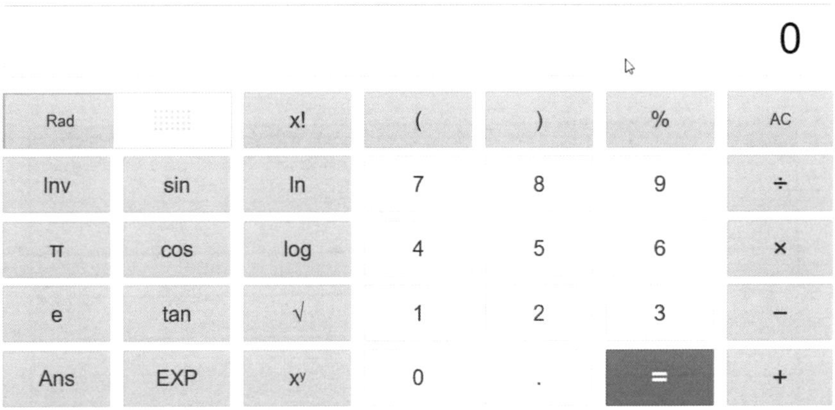

0

Rad	⠿	x!	(	)	%	AC
Inv	sin	ln	7	8	9	÷
π	cos	log	4	5	6	×
e	tan	√	1	2	3	−
Ans	EXP	xʸ	0	.	=	+

FIGURE 5.10

Calculator Syntax Example

UNIT CONVERTER

Unit converter will convert from one unit of measurement to another. Go to www.google.com. Once at the Google desktop, search the words "unit converter" (Figure 5.11).

FIGURE 5.11

Unit Converter Syntax Example

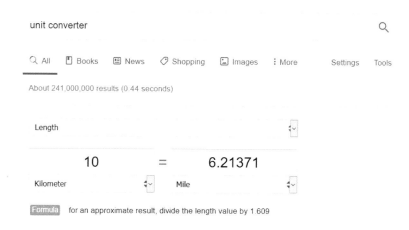

FIGURE 5.12

Social Versus Antisocial Syntax

Social Versus Antisocial Syntax

Google special syntax

Search operators that assist in more precise searching.

Social syntaxes or operators play well with other operators. These syntaxes can easily be mixed with other syntaxes to create the desired search results. Most of the Google special syntaxes are sociable. Antisocial syntaxes are search operators that do not combine with other operators and should be used individually (Figure 5.12).

Social Syntax	Antisocial Syntax
intitle:	define:
inurl:	link:
site:	calculator
intext:	unit converter
inanchor:	
filetype:	
related:	

Google News

The beautiful aspect of Google syntax is that these same operators work in Google News. If you want real-world news articles that pertain to your topic, then use Google Special Syntax in Google News. Your Google News search could be a keyword search, publication search, or location search (Google, 2018).

KEYWORD SEARCH

Example: intitle:"gun control"

If you search this term in Google News, the results will be current stories with gun control in the headlines.

PUBLICATION SEARCH

Example: site:ap.org

If you search this term in Google News, the results will be current news articles from the Associated Press.

LOCATION SEARCH

Example: Terrorism location:Syria

The third Google News search is location. If you search this term in Google News, the results will be current news articles about terrorism in Syria.

Bing Query Language

Bing Query Language, also called Bing Advanced Operator Syntax, contains search operators specially designed for the search engine Bing (www.bing.com). Many of the advanced operator syntaxes are similar to Google syntax. Despite the differences, the operation has the same effect in refining and searching with precision (Figure 5.13).

Bing query language

Also called Bing Advanced Operator Syntax. A search language that allows the user to refine search queries for more accurate searching.

FIGURE 5.13

Bing Query Language

Operator	Definition	Remarks	Example
altloc:	Used to specify a local search outside major markets.	The **altloc:** locations are derived from major markets for the given language (**pt-br** and **pt-pt**, in the case of this example).	lang:pt AND (altloc:br OR loc:br)
contains:	Keeps results focused on sites that have links to the file types you specify.		surfing contains:pdf
define:	Triggers an Instant Answer definition for the specified word.		define gravity
ext:	Returns web pages of the specified file name extension only.		surfing ext:pdf

continued...

feed:	Finds RSS (Really Simple Syndication) pertaining to the term you specify.	RSS (Really Simple Syndication) is a publishing format websites use to easily distribute, or syndicate content to a wide audience. You can add RSS feeds to an RSS reader to make finding news easier. Some RSS readers are web based, while other readers are separate downloads that run on your computer.	feed:surfing
filetype:	Returns only web pages of the specified file type.		surfing filetype:pdf
hasfeed:	Finds web pages that contain both the term or terms for which you are querying and one or more RSS or Atom feeds.		site:www.nytimes.com hasfeed:-surfing
inanchor:	Returns web pages that contain the specified term in the anchor text.	Word order is preserved; for example, **inanchor:bird watching** would search for **bird** before **watching** in anchor text.	inanchor:birdwatching
inbody:	Returns web pages that contain the specified term in the metadata or in the HTML body.	**Inbody:"spaces magog"** is a valid but different example, as it is a phrase match.	inbody:spaces inbody:magog
intitle:	Returns web pages that contain the specified term in the metadata title of the site.		intitle:surfing
location:	Returns web pages from a specific country or region. Specify the country or region code directly after the location: keyword.	This operator is not available for all languages. Same as the location:operator.	football location:ES
msite:	Source filtering used to refine a query for a multimedia site. Used for both **Image** and **Video** source types.		msite:hulu.com simpsons

site:	Returns web pages that belong to the specified site.	To focus on two or more domains, use OR to group the domains. You can use site: to search for web domains, top-level domains, and directories that are no more than two levels deep. You can also search for web pages that contain a specific search word on a site.	"heart disease" (site:bbc.co.uk OR site:cnn.com)
url:	Returns results that indicate whether the specified domain or URL is in the Bing Index.		url:microsoft.com

Summary

Usually a student's first place to begin research is via the Internet using Google or a favorite search engine. However, the first place for research should begin with your textbook. Textbooks are not just for reading. Mining references from the textbook is always a great place to begin because the subject and the support for literature are readily available. Implementing citation research allows the student to move backward and forward in time. Wikipedia can be used as a source for references to start research, but not as a credible source.

Employing Boolean language is the basis for Internet searching. To create more targeted searches, use Google Special Syntaxes and Bing Query Language.

Key Terms

Accuracy

Anchor

Bibliographic trail

Bibliography

Bing Query Language

Boolean searching

Citation indexing

Citations

File format

Flexible inclusion

Google Special Syntax

Nesting

Phrase searching

References

Sources

Temporal citations

Validity

Wikipedia

Wild cards

Seminal work

Syntax

Review Questions

1. Describe how a textbook should be used for research.
2. What does it mean to follow the bibliographic trail?
3. Identify and explain the difference between prospective and retrospective citations.
4. What is seminal work, and where would you find it?
5. List the uses for citation indexing.
6. How can Wikipedia be used as a starting point for research?
7. Why do instructors and academics advise students against the use of Wikipedia?
8. What are Boolean operators, and how are they used in Internet research?
9. What are operators, and how are they used in flexible inclusion?
10. Define nesting and its use in Internet research.
11. Define phrase search in Internet research.
12. What are wild cards, and how are they used?
13. What is Google Special Syntax, and how are search operands used in Internet research?
14. What are the top-level domains used on the Internet?
15. List and describe how each syntax is used to search the Internet.
16. Explain the difference between social and antisocial syntax.
17. Compare and contrast the search operands for Google versus Bing.
18. List tools used for Internet searches.

References

Athabasca University. (2017, August 8). *Research guides. tips for searching (Boolean Search Guide)*. Nesting. Retrieved from http://libguides.athabascau.ca/content.php?pid=48983&sid=360329

Azzam, A., Bresler, D., Leon, A., Maggio, L., Whitaker, E., Heilman, J., . . . McCue, J. D. (2017). Why medical schools should embrace wikipedia: Final-year medical student contributions to wikipedia articles for academic credit at one school. *Academic Medicine, 92*(2), 194–200. Retrieved from https://doi.org/10.1097/ACM.0000000000001381

Booth, W. C., Colomb, G. G., Williams, J. M., Bizup, J., & FitzGerald, W. T. (2016). *The craft of research* (4th ed.). Chicago, IL: University of Chicago Press.

Cathey, G. (2008, December 19). Basic Boolean search operators and query modifiers explained. Retrieved from http://booleanblackbelt.com/2008/12/basic-boolean-search-operators-and-query-modifiers-explained/

Dornfest, R., Bausch, P., & Calishain, T. (2006). *Google hacks: Tips & tools for finding and using the world's information* (3rd ed.). Sebastopol, CA: O'Reilly Media.

Google. (2018). *Search for news by keyword, site, or region—Computer—Google News Help.* Retrieved from https://support.google.com/news/answer/3334?co=GENIE.Platform%3DDesktop&hl=en

Huang, J., Shi, S., Chen, Y., & Chow, W. (2016). How do students trust Wikipedia? An examination across genders. *Information Technology & People*, 29(4), 750–773. Retrieved from https://doi.org/10.1108/ITP-12-2014-0267

Jemielniak, D., & Aibar, E. (2016). Bridging the gap between Wikipedia and academia. *Journal of the Association for Information Science and Technology*, 67(7), 1773–1776. Retrieved from https://doi.org/10.1002/asi.23691

Kousha, K., & Thelwall, M. (2017). Are Wikipedia citations important evidence of the impact of scholarly articles and books? *Journal of the Association for Information Science and Technology*, 68(3), 762–779. Retrieved from https://doi.org/10.1002/asi.23694

Merry, L. (2017, December 4). *Did you know anchors can help your website customers?* Retrieved from https://www.telegraph.co.uk/branded-content/marketing-guides/what-is-anchor-link/

Okoli, C., Mehdi, M., Mesgari, M., Nielsen, F. Å., & Lanamäki, A. (2014). Wikipedia in the eyes of its beholders: A systematic review of scholarly research on Wikipedia readers and readership. *Journal of the Association for Information Science & Technology*, 65(12), 2381–2403. Retrieved from https://doi.org/10.1002/asi.23162

CHAPTER 6

Finding the Tools for Research

Chapter Learning Objectives:

- Explain the CRAAAP method for evaluating research articles.
- Discuss the difference between aggregators and databases.
- Compare and contrast discovery searching versus federated searching.
- Discuss the features and benefits of federated and discovery searching.
- Discuss open-access journals.
- Discuss Google Scholar and its browser extension.
- Define and discuss academic blogs.

Search Systems in College Libraries

When researching at a college or university library, students must be seen as the primary stakeholder in their research efforts (Armstrong, 2009). Librarians are meant to guide students to the right resources to facilitate an efficient, productive search experience. The purpose of research is categorized into two main characteristics. First, research is a combined endeavor in which new knowledge is created based on an existing foundation of published studies. Second, collaboration is a key factor for scholars in different academic disciplines, allowing them to work together to solve problems. Research is an interdisciplinary and collaborative effort to solve problems (Becker, Heide, Knackstedt, & Steinhorst, 2013).

Peer-reviewed articles are research that is published in scholarly journals, mainly by academics. These articles are vetted. Other experts in the same field conduct the vetting process, in which the article is scrutinized for Currency, Relevance, Authority, Accuracy, Accessibility, and Purpose (CRAAAP). The CRAAAP information evaluation criteria have been adapted from the original work of Paula Hammett (1999). It allows for quick testing to uncover reliable information on the world wide web (Figure 6.1).

CRAAAP

Currency, Relevance, Authority, Accuracy, Accessibility, and Purpose.

FIGURE 6.1

Information Evaluation Criteria

Currency	Timeliness of the information	✓ When was the article published? ✓ Is the article current enough for your research?
Relevance	Importance of the information	✓ Does this information apply to your topic? ✓ Is this article suitable for your intended audience?
Authority	Source of the information	✓ What are the author's qualifications and credentials? ✓ Who is the publisher?
Accuracy	Reliability and validity of the information	✓ Is the information supported by evidence? ✓ Is it peer-reviewed?
Accessibility	Availability of the information	✓ Is the full text of the article available through your chosen library?
Purpose	Reason the information exist	✓ What is the thesis or purpose of the article? ✓ Does the article present a clear goal?

AGGREGATORS

aggregators

Online reference systems that license content from a wide variety of academic journals, books, periodicals, and primary sources.

Aggregators are online reference systems that license content from a wide variety of academic journals, books, periodicals, and primary sources. They house databases from leading academic material providers, such as JSTOR, Taylor & Francis, and SAGE Publications. The leading aggregators currently used today are EBSCO, ProQuest, and Cengage-**Gale**. These aggregators allow students and librarians a one-stop shopping place using federated and discovery searches.

Gale

Another aggregator that houses scholarly literature.

DATABASES

database

A repository of information that contains journal articles, newspapers, conference papers, magazines, and much more.

Aggregators house databases, which contain journals, articles, and other academic material needed to fulfill research needs. A **database** is an organized index of electronic information that allows a user to search for full-text academic journals, trade publications, conference proceedings, newspapers, magazines, industry reports, books, audiobooks, images, encyclopedias, dictionaries, videos, and more. Most of the information contained within a database is licensed proprietary information. So, the information obtained from a library database cannot be accessed on Internet search engines like Google or Yahoo. Using library databases, it is easy to identify scholarly sources because the information has already been carefully vetted for credibility and accuracy (Figure 6.2).

Aggregators	EBSCOhost	ProQuest	Cengage-Gale
Database Examples	• Academic Search Complete • Business Source Complete • CINAHL Complete • EconLit with Full Text • Education Source • Entrepreneurial Studies Source • ERIC • MasterFILE Premier • MEDLINE Complete	• ABI/INFORM • JSTOR • PsycARTICLES • PsycINFO • PsycEXTRA • Accounting, Tax & Banking Collection	• InfoTrac • Academic OneFile • Business Insights: Global • Business Economics and Theory Collection
Journal Examples	• *Leadership Quarterly* • *Journal of Marketing*	• *Academy of Strategic Management Journal* • *Business Process Management Journal*	• *Academy of Information and Management Sciences Journal* • *Academy of Entrepreneurship Journal*

Databases allow users to search by keyword or subject. Most searches begin with keywords, then are refined using the aggregator's filtering features. Advanced searches contain drop-down menus that allow users to customize the search. Many students state it is difficult to use databases and they cannot find information. Well, certain databases cater to a particular discipline. For example, a student would not use a psychology database to search for a business article and journal. When in doubt about what database to use, ask a librarian. Librarians are there to assist you in finding the right database for your academic discipline or topic.

FIGURE 6.2

Aggregators and Databases

Information Discovery

FEDERATED SEARCHING

Federated searching allows the user to retrieve information from multiple sources, namely databases from a single-entry point, which facilitates a list of common results based on keyword or Boolean searching (Korah & Cassidy, 2010). Performing a federated search connects the user to multidisciplinary databases that would normally be searched one by one. The results of a federated search will appear as hyperlinks that connect directly to multiple library catalogs, subscription resources, and databases (Deshmukh, Bhavsar, & Bhavsar, 2012). Federated searching within a college library gives the user access to information that would not normally be found during a web search because of secure access. One of the main benefits of federated searching is locating databases that are best for a particular discipline (Georgas, 2013). Other benefits of federated searching are

federated searching

Allows the user to retrieve information from multiple sources, namely databases from a single-entry point.

reduced search time; the ability to refine, save, email, and export content; and easy-to-view results. The aggregators EBSCOhost, ProQuest, and Cengage-Gale use federated search technology to allow users to reduce the amount of research time and have access to diverse information sources that give integrated search results.

EBSCOHOST

EBSCO

Elton B. Stephens Company is a leading aggregator; EBSCOhost provides full-text access to thousands of periodicals and peer-reviewed journals.

EBSCO (Elton B. Stephens Company) is accessed through a college or public library. EBSCOhost provides full-text access to thousands of periodicals and peer-reviewed journals. EBSCO supports Boolean search logic (discussed in Chapter 5) and directs readers to relevant research in a variety of fields (Figure 6.3). The basic search uses keywords from your topic, whereas the advanced search uses Guided Style fields to assist the user in creating a relevant and targeted search. Guided Style fields are limiters that help in reducing search results, targeting information more efficiently.

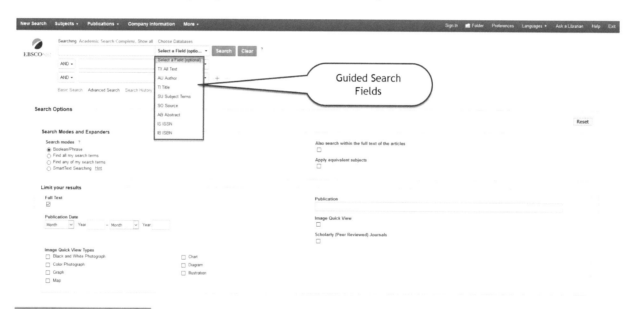

FIGURE 6.3

EBSCOhost Database Search

Boolean searching assists in refining research topics. Additionally, limiters can narrow search parameters for full-text scholarly work. Many students find it difficult to use because of the massive amount of information EBSCO offers. The first step in conquering EBSCO is to register for a free username and password (Figure 6.4). By creating an EBSCO account, all researched information can be saved for future use. In addition, a user can share research and create Really Simple Syndication (RSS) feeds by creating a free username and password.

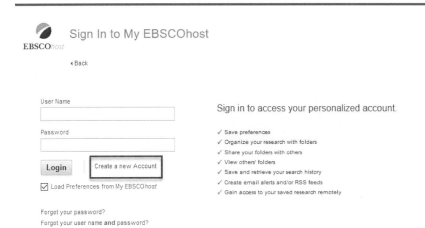

FIGURE 6.4

Free Username and Password

EBSCO features include formatting citations within articles to assist in creating a properly cited reference page or bibliography (Figure 6.5).

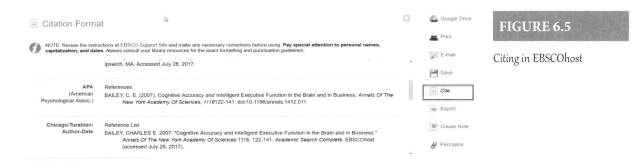

FIGURE 6.5

Citing in EBSCOhost

Exporting articles to bibliographic managers, emailing articles for collaborative learning, sharing articles on social media, creating notes for annotation, saving documents to Google Drive, or just plain old printing hard copy are all features and benefits that make EBSCOhost's federated searching appealing to researchers. In addition, RSS feeds allow you to create alerts when topics from a favorite journal become available.

EBSCO also offers an app for accessing EBSCOhost from your iOS (iPhone, iPod Touch, and iPad) and Android devices. The EBSCOhost app is available for download from the Apple App Store as well as Google Play.

PROQUEST

ProQuest

Leading aggregator that houses full-text coverage of thousands of periodicals and peer-reviewed journals.

ProQuest is a top competitor of EBSCOhost and is an impressive aggregator or database search application that can be accessed through any college library. ProQuest includes full-text coverage of thousands of periodicals and peer-reviewed journals. Like EBSCOhost, ProQuest provides relevant, multidisciplinary resources. ProQuest is also very student-friendly. Its services enable the user to satisfy almost any informational need. Before researching within Pro-Quest, create a "My Research Account," which is a free username and password. Having your own account has many benefits, such as:

- Saving searches and researched documents, which can be stored for years
- Creating folders for easy document management
- Creating RSS feeds
- Collaborating through email and social media connections

Many of these features are the same as EBSCOhost's; however, ProQuest owns the bibliographic manager RefWorks, which synchronizes with "My Research" for exporting all saved research. Another feature of ProQuest is the ability to create a reference page from saved research. This is easy. All the user must do is select all of the research found and click **Cite** to create a properly formatted reference page in different citation styles. See Figure 6.6.

FIGURE 6.6

Citing in ProQuest

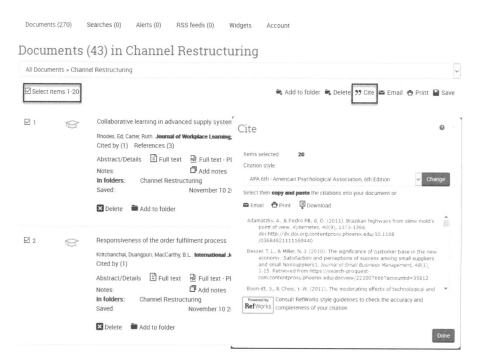

Using the cite feature, ProQuest acts as a mini reference manager. Chapter 7 of this book discusses reference managers in detail.

When using ProQuest, there are five types of searches:

1. Basic Search: Search by using keywords or phrases. This feature allows Boolean searching.
2. Advanced Search: Use a search form customized with search field and ProQuest-specific search-operator drop-downs (Figure 6.7).

FIGURE 6.7

Using ProQuest Limiters

3. Command Line Search: Search multiple fields using Pro-Quest field codes and Boolean operators. You can do this in the advanced-search drop-down box, but experienced researchers prefer this method because it allows for a more precise search (Figure 6.7.1). Example: SU leadership AND (TI charismatic OR (TI motivation AND TI transformational))

   SU is "subject" and TI is "title." This search looks at the subject of leadership and searches for "charismatic" or "motivation and transformational" in the title of each article (Vasut, 2016).

FIGURE 6.7.1

Using ProQuest Limiters Command Line Search

4. Publication Search: Users can search and locate various publications within the ProQuest database. Each library will have a different subscription level, so not every library will carry the same publications (Figure 6.7.2).

FIGURE 6.7.2

ProQuest Publication Search

ProQuest does not have an app to search its extensive databases. However, ProQuest does have an eBook app called Bluefire. The Bluefire eBook reader reads Adobe Content Server–protected eBooks.

Discovery Searching

discovery searching

A unified index source for searching. Only searches one large database, not multiple, to increase the speed of searching.

Discovery searching is the vendor's answer to the competition from Google. By creating a unified search index, discovery search addresses the need for a simple interface, similar to Google, for accessing library resources. Many users found federated search slow and cumbersome. Students wanted more power and speed when searching for scholarly material. Discovery tools simultaneously search multiple databases and library content from a single search box to locate scholarly material without having to search various places on library databases. Breeding (2010) described discovery tools as a "blending of the full text of journal articles and books alongside citation data, bibliographic, and authority records resulting in a powerful search experience" (p. 33).

Unlike federated searching, discovery searching does not expect the user to possess research literacy. Discovery empowers the user to search a large variety of information from a single entry point. Using a discovery service, many users find identifying library materials from catalogs, publishers, aggregators with a Google-like feel (Burke & Tumbleson, 2016). Discovery searching identifies all library holdings in one database. A discovery service may include catalog records, indexes and databases, research guides, web pages, and open-access content. The main advantage and difference between federated searching and discovery searching is the information in discovery searching is preharvested. Preharvested information allows information to be accumulated and processed in advance of searches (Asher, Duke, & Wilson, 2013; Das, 2015). Data is collected from multiple sources and processed into a central index. Again, these services give the user access to all library collections, regardless of its physical or electronic location. Discovery tools break down silos that are created with traditional databases (Figure 6.8).

Features	Benefits
Single search and speed	Provides a Google-like search experience, allowing the user to use one search box to ascertain credible content with instant results
Relevant content results	Delivers result that are ranked and relevant based on keyword search
Complete and instant access	Complete and comprehensive access to full-text library holdings
Access to critical subject's indexes	Provides access via platform blending and combines rich metadata with subject indexing and abstracts from leading subject indexes
Mobile accessibility	Accesses library holdings from any mobile device
Results refinement	Search results can be narrowed and refined by using multiple methods, such as filtering, faceting (use of multiple categorical filters), and sorting
Citation formatting	Generates citations in the required style, such as APA, MLA, or Chicago
Bibliographic information export	Exports citations to bibliographic managers such as RefWorks or EndNote
Sharing and collaboration	Shares information through email, RSS feeds, and social media

FIGURE 6.8

Major Features and Benefits of Discovery Searches

The major discovery products used within college, university, and state library systems are EBSCO Discovery Service, Summon from ProQuest, WorldCat Discovery, and Ex Libris' Primo (Figure 6.9).

Aggregator/vendor name	Product name	Website
ProQuest	Summon	www.proquest.com/products-services/discovery-services/The-Summon-Service.html
EBSCO	Discovery Service	www.ebscohost.com/discovery
ProQuest Ex Libris'	Primo	www.exlibrisgroup.com/category/PrimoOverview
OCLC	WorldCat Discovery	www.oclc.org/en/worldcat-discovery.html

WorldCat

World Catalog. A library catalog where information is discovered globally.

Ex Libris

Academic database owned by ProQuest.

FIGURE 6.9

Discovery Tools

Online Computer Library Center (OCLC)

The Online Computer Library Center is a global library cooperative where libraries worldwide are members.

PROQUEST SUMMON

Use Summon to search across the library collection.

Q   Search for articles, books, and more

SEARCH

ProQuest Summon is a discovery search engine that provides access to scholarly material using a single Google-like search box (Figure 6.10). Through Summon, users can find journal articles, books, newspapers, conference papers, and dissertations in the college library collection simultaneously. Summon allows a variety of search options that allow the user to gain familiarity with database searching (Ex Libris, 2016a, 2016b). Other search features of Summon's are:

- Phrase searches limit results to exact phrase matches. Summon uses this feature to increase what they call the "verbatim match boost," increasing the number of matched results due to exact phrasing.
- Field searches limit results to matches in the specified fields, such as title, author, or subject terms. Examples include *Title:(Charismatic Leadership), Title:(Barriers to Entry), Author:(Jay Conger), SubjectTerms:(Business Programs)*.
- Boolean searches, depending on how they are written, can either limit or expand your search. In Summon, Boolean search operators must be written in capital letters (AND, BUT, OR) for proper interpretation.
- Wildcard searches expand your searches based on word stems or spelling variations. Two wildcards are recognized by Summon: the question mark (?) and the asterisk (*). The question mark (?) will match any one character. Example: Ba?er will return results with the name Baker or Bauer (Figure 6.11).

The asterisk (*) will match zero or more characters within a word or at the end of a word. Example: Temp* results will yield results as shown in Figure 6.12. These results include the word "temperature." Placing the asterisk at the end of the word will allow all possible characters to be included in the search results.

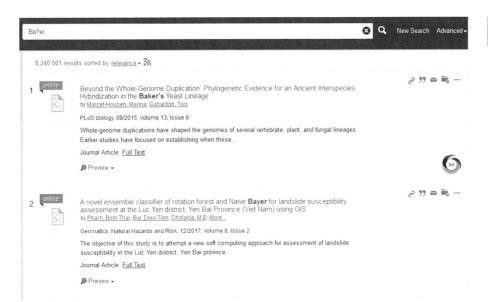

FIGURE 6.11

Search Syntax (?)

FIGURE 6.12

Search Syntax (*)

- Proximity searches limit results to terms that appear within a specified number of words in a phrase. To perform a proximity search, enclose your search terms in quotation marks and use the tilde (~) followed by a number indicating the distance you want to allow between the search terms. For example, "strategic management"~10 finds material where "strategic" and "management" appear within ten words of each other (Figure 6.13).

Summon also has the "database recommendations" feature, which will generate a list of recommended databases from your college library holdings that allow a more focused search of the chosen topic. Additionally, the user can "Add results beyond your library's collection." This feature will include the entire Summon index and open-access records.

EBSCO DISCOVERY

EBSCO Discovery is a direct competitor of ProQuest Summon. Known as the next-generation search engine, EBSCO Discovery has all the features of EBSCO-host with additional exciting ones such as using a single search box to begin your research. According to EBSCO, their search engine contains information from seventy thousand publishers with hundreds of thousands of journals, articles, books, and magazines (EBSCO Information Services, 2016).

With intuitive features such as SmartLinks to full text, full-text language translation, RSS feeds, and email alerts, EBSCO Discovery allows for precision searching that saves users time. EBSCO Discovery works on mobile devices such as smartphones and tablets. Researchers will not have to relearn EBSCO Discovery if they are already proficient in EBSCOhost, as the same basic rules apply. Another popular feature is Research Starter. Research Starter is designed to aid users in locating authoritative articles on popular and controversial topics, and it uses metadata as the key enabler for basic discovery searches.

Portals and Open-Source Discovery Tools

Portals are customized and integrated doorways to various information resources, services, and websites on the Internet through a single access point (Al-Dossari, 2017; Burke & Tumbleson, 2016; Masrek, Jamaludin, & Mukhtar, 2010). A portal allows the researcher to enter a gateway to find targeted information and improve the quality of results. The main reason portals exist is to encourage collaboration, manage knowledge, and disseminate research (Becker et al., 2013; Becker, Knackstedt, Lis, Stein, & Steinhorst, 2012).

portals

Customized and integrated doorways to various information resources, services, and websites through a single access point.

Portals promote and strengthen virtual research communities, which allows for internal communication and the transfer of knowledge between the author and the research. Accessing portals gives the student-researcher a powerful tool for improving the quality and content of an academic paper. Colleges and universities are now creating portals to enhance the student learning process. Some portals link to a college library holding across various disciplines. Google Scholar and Microsoft Academic are portals that students and researchers often use.

Open access grants the user free access to view, read, and download digital academic content (Rowlands & Nicholas, 2008). **Open-access journals** are a great resource for students to freely enhance their knowledge about a topic without using commercial Internet sources. Additionally, open-access databases satisfy the "Internet-first" response that most students have acquired due to convenience.

open-access journals

?

DIRECTORY OF OPEN-ACCESS JOURNALS (DOAJ)

The **Directory of Open-Access Journals** (www.doaj.org) consists of free, peer-reviewed, no-embargo articles that are immediately available online as soon as they are published. The goal of the DOAJ is to boost the visibility and increase the accessibility of scholarly journals. According to Crawford (2015), the DOAJ is the best portal for accessing open-access journals across all scholarly disciplines. Approximately 27 percent of all peer-reviewed scholarly journals are listed in the DOAJ. The DOAJ is sustained by aggregators, librarians, individuals, scholarly communities, library associations, and service providers.

Directory of Open-Access Journal

Consists of free, peer-reviewed, no-embargo articles that are immediately available online as soon they are published.

The DOAJ has comprehensive coverage, including (1) scientific and scholarly research topics, (2) peer-reviewed journals, articles, and periodicals, (3) government, commercial, and nonprofit publications, and (4) publications in different languages (Thavamani, 2013).

User navigation and searching

The home page of the DOAJ has a basic search-box feature similar to a search engine (Figure 6.14). Like federated and discovery searching, basic keywords can be limited to journals or articles. The right-hand side of the screen illustrates basic statistics such as the number of accessible journals and articles, frequently asked questions, information about open-access journals, best practices, new journal RSS feeds, and metadata information for publishers. Social media–sharing tools (Twitter, Facebook, Google+) are found on the right side of the page (Morrison, 2017).

FIGURE 6.14

DOAJ Home Page

The advanced search feature allows users to use search limiters to narrow search results. Limiters are designated fields such as keyword, title, subject, language, or year that allow users to easily filter and find the right results. Users can share embedded links to place articles on social media, share through email, or place on a web page (Figure 6.15).

FIGURE 6.15

DOAJ Search

The ability to click on the title of the article is another advanced feature of the DOAJ. By clicking on the journal name, users receive detailed information about the journal. Features include the journal name, a link to the journal, full text, and the abstract. Other features include information and instructions for authors (Figure 6.16).

FIGURE 6.16

DOAJ Journal Information

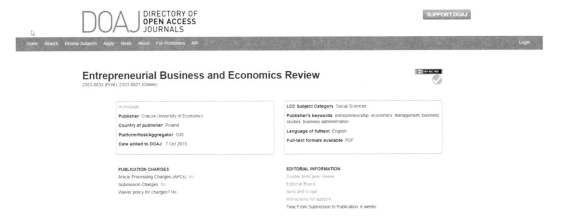

GOOGLE SCHOLAR

Google Scholar (scholar.google.com) is a free multidisciplinary academic discovery tool that enables the user to search for scholarly literature. It offers research-management support that helps the user organize and manage research findings. Google Scholar provides a one-stop search location for academic scholarly resources. It is an excellent tool for topic searches (Ciccone & Vickery, 2015), which helps students transition from being web searchers to scholarly searchers (Wenzler, 2013). Users have the ability to search for a wide variety of peer-reviewed papers, theses, books, conference papers, patents, and legal proceedings from colleges, universities, and other organizations that publish scholarly, academic material (Google, n.d.). Google Scholar empowers the student-researcher by quickly identifying relevant scholarly sources, including documentation in PDF, Microsoft Word, or PowerPoint file types. For nonacademic writers or the novice researcher, Google Scholar is an excellent starting point for the research process (Ettinger, 2007; Kent, 2005). As a discovery tool, Google Scholar is an ally for the student-researcher because full-text access to library collections and vendor collections become more visible.

Google Scholar

Free multidisciplinary academic discovery tool that enables the user to search for scholarly literature. Provides a one-stop search location for academic scholarly resources.

Before you use Google Scholar

It is recommended that a user create a Gmail account before using Google Scholar. Gmail interfaces with Google Scholar, allowing the user to fully access the features and benefits it offers. For example, having an account allows you to create a Google Scholar profile if you decide to publish, save research, or create alerts. It is also recommended that you use a personal Gmail account and not a professional, institutional, or school email so your account has a sense of permanency and follows you wherever you go.

Basic search

Google Scholar begins with a simple search box. To begin, enter a keyword or words into the search box, the same as if you were using the Google search engine. Google Scholar will return inquiry results with limiters to narrow your search by year, date, patents, or citations relevant to the search. A basic search will also allow you to create alerts based on the search query.

Basic search queries include Boolean searches as discussed in Chapter 5. In addition, Google Special Syntax can be used within Google Scholar; this will help you get the most out of Google Scholar before using advanced search features. On the search results page, limiters can be found to assist in narrowing search results (Figure 6.17).

FIGURE 6.17

Google Scholar Desktop

FIGURE 6.18

Google Scholar Basic Search

Figure 6.18 shows the results of a basic search. The basic search illustrates additional information such as:

1. Cited by: This refers to the number of authors who have cited this article in their own work. In Figure 6.19, the "cited by" count is 3,019, which is a popular article that many authors have cited within their own work. It also serves as a temporal citation, allowing you to move forward in time. Also,

once a researcher clicks **Cited by** for their chosen article, at this point they can search only within the citing articles.

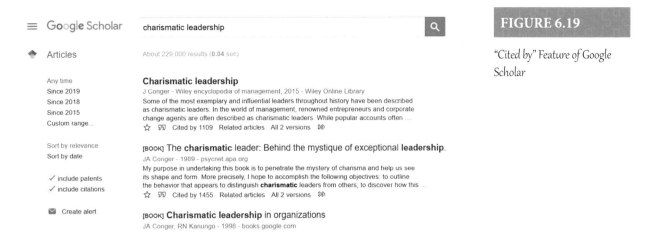

FIGURE 6.19

"Cited by" Feature of Google Scholar

2. Related articles: This feature allows the user to retrieve articles that are similar to the search result (Figure 6.20).

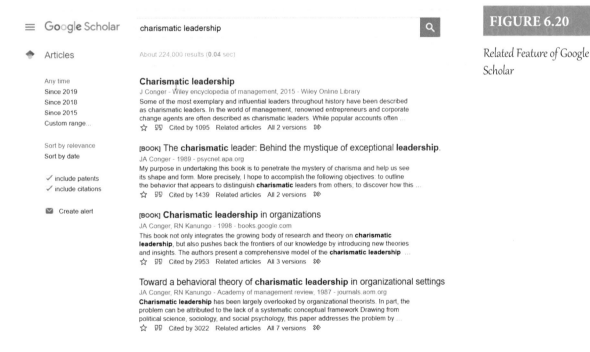

FIGURE 6.20

Related Feature of Google Scholar

3. Versions: Sometimes, an article is available in more than one file format or source location. If more than one format is available, Google Scholar provides the necessary information and locates all versions of the chosen article through hyperlinks. This is a unique feature of Google Scholar (Figure 6.21).

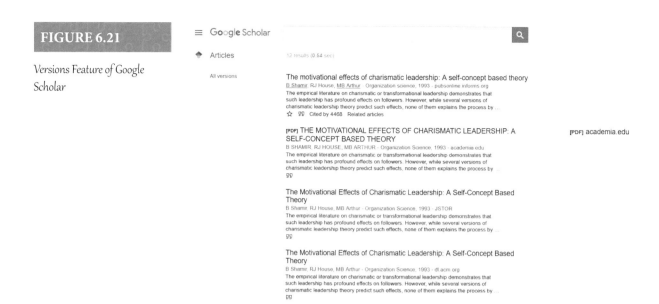

FIGURE 6.21

Versions Feature of Google Scholar

4. Cite: Many students have trouble creating a good reference page. Arranging citations takes time and experience, but Google Scholar assists in creating solid citations and references. By clicking on **Cite**, it creates a formatted citation for the chosen research article. Google Scholar provides citations in MLA, APA, Chicago, Harvard, and Vancouver format (Figure 6.22). Additionally, users can export the citation into bibliographic reference managers such as EndNote, RefWorks, or Zotero.

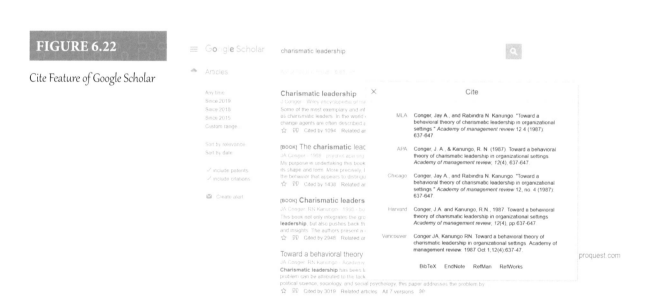

FIGURE 6.22

Cite Feature of Google Scholar

5. Save: This allows the user to save research articles into "My Library" for reading at a later date. To use the save feature, the user must have a Gmail account. By saving articles, search results can be archived for future use (Figure 6.23).

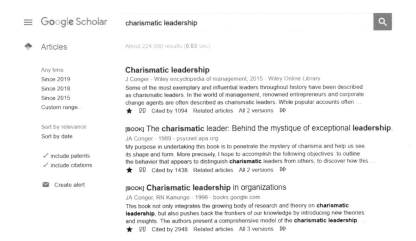

6. More: This advanced search feature shown in Figure 6.24 is directly connected to library links, allowing the user to search multiple library catalogs at the same time.

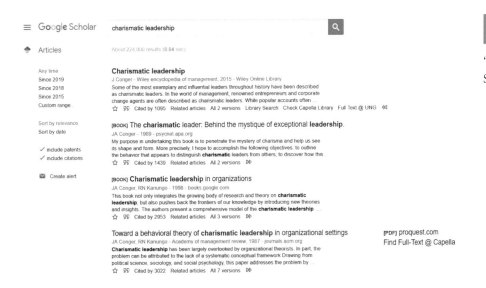

Advanced search

To access some of the advanced features of Google Scholar, log in using Gmail. Advanced search allows you to search using Boolean logic. On the main Google

Scholar desktop, the drop-down arrow at the right of the search box will allow access to advanced search. To use advanced search, you fill in the requested information within the digital form. This completes the metadata, or the information about the author, publisher, date, or title. Using advanced search lets you access single publications for a particular author (Figure 6.25).

FIGURE 6.25

Advanced Search Feature of Google Scholar

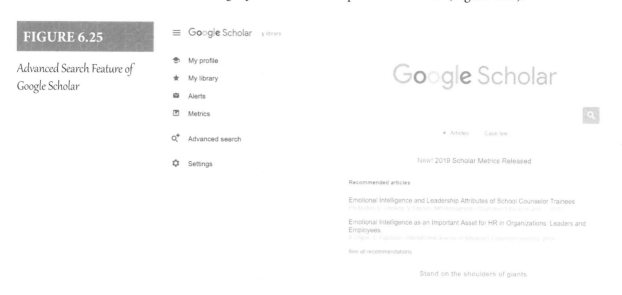

Google Scholar settings

Settings allow the user to customize Google Scholar to become more user-friendly (Figure 6.26).

FIGURE 6.26

Settings in Google Scholar

KEY TOOLS OF WRITING AND RESEARCH *A Guide for the Student Writer*

Search results

The search results settings allow the user to change the search results per page. Ten search results are automatically provided. However, the user can see a maximum of twenty results per page. One of the most important features of search results is importing found research into a bibliographic manager. Links can be shown if bibliographic or reference managers are used (Figure 6.27).

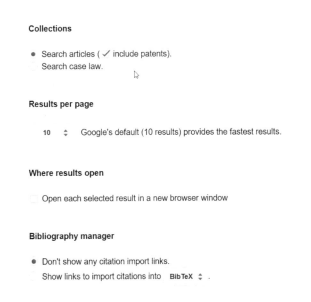

FIGURE 6.27

Managing Search Results in Google Scholar

Languages

Google Scholar has language support. The user can search for research articles in any written language or a specific language. By default, Google Scholar retrieves information in all languages. The language setting allows you to restrict this feature to one or more languages. This feature is excellent for dual-language speakers (Figure 6.28).

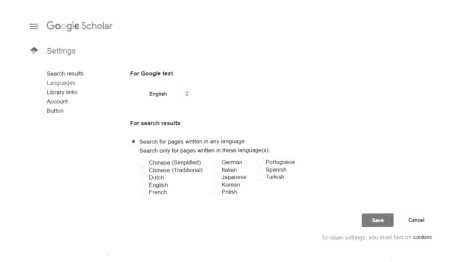

FIGURE 6.28

Languages Setting of Google Scholar

LIBRARY LINKS

Library links allows the user to connect to a college library's electronic and print holdings. Now you are searching your college library's holdings and Google Scholar simultaneously. For large research projects, the library links setting saves time (Figure 6.29).

GOOGLE SCHOLAR BUTTON

The Google Scholar button is a browser extension that allows you to find full-text articles from common Internet searches or a college library. The Google Scholar button has the ability to transform a normal Google search into a scholarly search within a matter of seconds. This is an excellent quick scholarly search tool with the following benefits:

- Quickly searches Google Scholar
- Automatically checks for full-text articles
- Provides citation information
- Provides library link if set up through Google Scholar
- Provides quick citation link
- Provides "cited by" count
- Provides link to related articles
- Formats references in the major citation styles

Once the Google Scholar extension is installed, press the Google Scholar button in a browser such as Google Chrome or Firefox (Lazyscholar, 2015) (Figures 6.30 and 6.31).

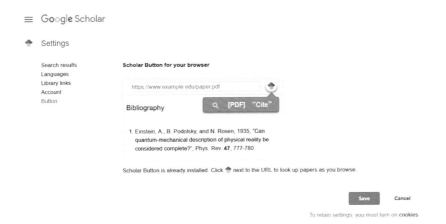

FIGURE 6.30

Google Scholar Button for Internet Browser

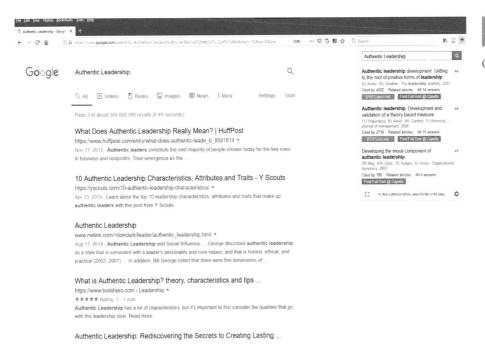

FIGURE 6.31

Google Scholar Button Example

MICROSOFT ACADEMIC

Microsoft Academic (academic.microsoft.com) has been revamped as of July 2017. Like Google Scholar, Microsoft Academic is a search engine that uses keyword search to find scholarly literature. It provides recommendations and related results to assist the researcher in discovering more scholarly articles of interest. Microsoft Query Language and keyword searching can be used to improve search results. Once search results are obtained, users have the ability to download PDF documents when available, share on social media, or cite in APA, MLA, or Chicago style. Another exciting feature of Microsoft Academic is transferring citations into Microsoft Word, which acts as a mini bibliographic manager. See Chapter 7 for more details on reference managers. You can sign in using

Microsoft Academic

Microsoft Academic is a scholarly search engine that uses keyword search to find scholarly literature.

your Microsoft, Google, or Facebook account. Currently, Microsoft Academic does have the ability to save found articles through reading list once signed into your account. Finally, Microsoft Academic is a viable academic search engine for the researcher's toolbox (Figure 6.32).

Name	Website	Information
CiteSeerX	citeseerx.ist.psu.edu/index	Free public academic search engine and digital library
RefSeek	www.refseek.com	Web search engine for students and researchers that aims to make academic information easily accessible to everyone; searches more than one billion documents, including web pages, books, encyclopedias, journals, and newspapers
Semantic Scholar	www.semanticscholar.org	Free academic search engine
Wolfram Alpha	www.wolframalpha.com	The computational search engine

academic blogs

Also known as weblogs, blogs contain scholarly, peer-reviewed articles and journals.

blog

Online diary or journal on a website, also called weblog.

convergence

Allows an author to share research through blog posting, extend its shelf life, and make it accessible to nonspecialists.

scholarly blog

Also known as academic blogs, they contain scholarly, peer-reviewed articles and journals.

Academic Blogs

Blogs or weblogs are online diaries or journals. They can contain the author's opinions, experiences, and insights. Blogs are online conversations that allow readers to express opinions about a subject and take conversations beyond a textbook or article. For example, researchers can now tell the backstory of their research. **Convergence** is practiced once a book is placed on a website. Convergence allows an author to share research through blogs, videos, and personal contact online, which extends a book's shelf life and makes it accessible to non-specialists. Users seeking out blogs practice selective exposure, meaning they regularly look for messages that correspond to their own social convictions, qualities, and research interests (Campbell, Martin, & Fabos, 2011). **Scholarly blogs**, however, are difficult to locate. A search for scholarly blogs can be performed through www.blogsearchengine.org/, although this might not yield the desired result.

PROQUEST: ACI SCHOLARLY BLOG INDEX

The ACI Scholarly Blog Index is the only scholarly blog search engine on the Internet covering the fields of humanities, science, and social science. Its purpose is to evaluate and then index scholarly blogs for undergraduates, graduates, faculty, and researchers. The ACI indexes over ten thousand blogs and over one million posts with close-to-real-time RSS feeds (Figure 6.33). "ProQuest has agreed to license and include all of the full-text content contained in the ACI Scholarly Blog Index so that the academic and research communities can continue to easily access the curated collection of blogs written by academic scholars" (ACI, 2018, para. 1).

Free Scholarly Blog Discovery Services		
Research Blogging	researchblogging.org	Indexes blog posts containing peer-reviewed research. Each post relates to a peer-reviewed journal article.
AllTop	alltop.com	"Personal online magazine rack" of your favorite websites and blogs, once you create a free username and password
Feedly	feedly.com	RSS feed aggregator service that manages blogs

FIGURE 6.33

Other Free Scholarly Blog Discovery Services

Scholarly blogs can increase your understanding of the research, and how and why it is performed. A blog can be considered an open invitation to learning (Deitering & Gronemyer, 2011; Kjellberg, 2014; Whitt, 2017).

Summary

Locating the right tools for research is a tough task for most student writers. Where do you find the necessary information to write without using Google? Chapter 6 introduced federated and discovery searching using ProQuest and EBSCO, and discussed the use of open-access journals, which are free scholarly articles open to the public. Google Scholar is an open-research portal that allows students to search their college library holdings and Google Scholar at the same time. To increase Internet browser function, the Google Scholar browser button allows students to search the Internet and link with Google Scholar. Knowing the right research tools is critical to the process of locating literature that supports your thesis, outline, and final paper.

Key Terms

Academic blogs
Aggregators
Blogs
Convergence
CRAAAP
Database

Directory of Open-
    Access Journals
Discovery searching
EBSCO
Ex Libris
Federated searching

Gale
Google Scholar
Microsoft Academic
OCLC
Open-access journals
Portals

ProQuest
Scholarly blog
WorldCat

Review Questions

1. How are research articles evaluated? Summarize each criterion.
2. What are aggregators, and how are they used in research?
3. Compare and contrast federated searching versus discovery searching.
4. What are the features and benefits of EBSCOhost?
5. What are the features and benefits of ProQuest?
6. What is a portal, and how can it be used in academic research?
7. Define and discuss open access.
8. Based on what you know about discovery searching, how would you use the tools presented in the chapter for your own research?
9. Identify the features and benefits of Google Scholar.
10. How would you use Google Scholar to support your research?

References

ACI. (2018, June 18). *ACI Scholarly Blog Index has been discontinued*. Retrieved from https://aci.info/discontinued/

Al-Dossari, H. (2017). A heuristic-based approach for usability evaluation of academic portals. *International Journal of Computer Science & Information Technology, 9*(3), 16. Retrieved from https://doi.org/10.5121/ijcsit.2017.9302

Armstrong, A. R. (2009). Student perceptions of federated searching vs single database searching. *Reference Services Review, 37*(3), 291–303. Retrieved from https://doi.org/10.1108/00907320910982785

Asher, A. D., Duke, L. M., & Wilson, S. (2013). Paths of discovery: comparing the search effectiveness of EBSCO Discovery Service, Summon, Google Scholar, and Conventional Library Resources. *College & Research Libraries, 74*(5), 464–488. Retrieved from https://doi.org/10.5860/crl-374

Becker, J., Heide, T., Knackstedt, R., & Steinhorst, M. (2013). Supporting knowledge management and collaboration in research communities using automatically created research portals. *International Journal of Web Portals (IJWP), 5*(2), 1–16. Retrieved from https://doi.org/10.4018/jwp.2013040101

Becker, J., Knackstedt, R., Lis, L., Stein, A., & Steinhorst, M. (2012). Research portals: Status quo and improvement perspectives. *International Journal of Knowledge Management (IJKM), 8*(3), 27–46. Retrieved from https://doi.org/10.4018/jkm.2012070102

Breeding, M. (2010). The state of the art in library discovery 2010. *Computers in Libraries; Westport, 30*(1), 31–34.

Burke, J. J., & Tumbleson, B. E. (2016). Chapter 3. Search systems and finding tools. *Library Technology Reports, 52*(2), 17–22. Retrieved from https://journals.ala.org/index.php/ltr/article/view/5911

Campbell, R., Martin, C. R., & Fabos, B. (2011). *Media and culture: An introduction to mass communication* (8th ed.). Boston, MA: Bedford/St. Martin's.

Ciccone, K., & Vickery, J. (2015). Summon, EBSCO Discovery Service, and Google Scholar: A comparison of search performance using user queries. *Evidence Based Library and Information Practice, 10*(1), 34–49. Retrieved from https://doi.org/10.18438/B86G6Q

Crawford, W. (2015). Dealing with OA Journals. *Library Technology Reports, 51*(6), 32–35.

Das, A. K. (2015). Information retrieval and search process in web-scale discovery tools. *E-Library Science Research Journal, 3*(8), 1–14. Retrieved from https://pdfs.semanticscholar.org/0609/de3594baee273766af5610a3d7417a86f985.pdf

Deitering, A. M., & Gronemyer, K. (2011). Beyond peer-reviewed articles: Using blogs to enrich students' understanding of scholarly work. *Portal: Libraries and the Academy; Baltimore, 11*(1), 489–503.

Deshmukh, S., Bhavsar, S., & Bhavsar, S. (2012). Open source software for federated search. *DESIDOC Journal of Library & Information Technology; Delhi, 32*(5). Retrieved from https://doi.org/10.14429/djlit.32.5.2647

EBSCO Information Services. (2016, June 2). *EBSCO discovery service (EDS)—Information sheet*. Retrieved from https://help.ebsco.com/interfaces/EBSCO_Discovery_Service/EDS_FAQs/EDS_Information_Sheet

Ettinger, D. (2007). The triumph of expediency: The impact of Google Scholar on library instruction. *Journal of Library Administration, 46*(3–4), 65–72. Retrieved from https://doi.org/10.1300/J111v46n03_06

Ex Libris. (2016a, September 3). Summon: Add results beyond your library's collection. Retrieved from https://knowledge.exlibrisgroup.com/Summon/Product_Documentation/Searching_in_The_Summon_Service/Search_Features/Summon%3A_Add_Results_Beyond_Your_Library's_Collection

Ex Libris. (2016b, September 3). *Summon: Phrase, field, Boolean, wildcard and proximity searching*. Retrieved from https://knowledge.exlibrisgroup.com/Summon/Product_Documentation/Searching_in_The_Summon_Service/Search_Features/Summon%3A_Boolean%2C_Phrase%2C_Wildcard_and_Proximity_Searching

Georgas, H. (2013). Google vs. the library: Student preferences and perceptions when doing research using Google and a federated search tool. *Portal: Libraries and the Academy; Baltimore, 13*(2), 165–185. Retrieved from https://doi.org/10.1353/pla.2013.0011

Hammett, P. (1999). Teaching tools for evaluating World Wide Web resources. *Teaching Sociology, 27*(1), 31–37. Retrieved from https://www.jstor.org/stable/1319243

Kent, M. L. (2005). Conducting better research: Google scholar and the future of search technology. *Public Relations Quarterly, 50*(4), 35.

Kjellberg, S. (2014). Researchers' blogging practices in two epistemic cultures: The scholarly blog as a situated genre. *Human IT: Journal for Information Technology Studies as a Human Science, 12*(3), 36–77. Retrieved from https://humanit.hb.se/article/view/474

Korah, A., & Cassidy, E. D. (2010). Students and federated searching: A survey of use and satisfaction. *Reference & User Services Quarterly, 49*(4), 325–332. Retrieved from https://www.jstor.org/stable/20865293

Lazyscholar. (2015, April 11). *Google Scholar Button vs. Lazy Scholar*. Retrieved from http://www.lazyscholar.org/2015/04/11/google-scholar-button-vs-lazy-scholar/

Masrek, M., Jamaludin, A., & Mukhtar, S. (2010). Evaluating academic library portal effectiveness: A Malaysian case study. *Library Review, 59*(3), 198–212. Retrieved from https://doi.org/10.1108/00242531011031188

Morrison, H. (2017). Directory of open-access journals (DOAJ). *The Charleston Advisor, 18*(3), 25–28. Retrieved from https://doi.org/10.5260/chara.18.3.25

Rowlands, I., & Nicholas, D. (2008). Open-access journals. In *The International Encyclopedia of Communication*. American Cancer Society. Retrieved from https://doi.org/10.1002/9781405186407.wbieco009

Thavamani, K. (2013). Directory of Open Access Journals: A bibliometric study of library and information science. *Collaborative Librarianship, 5*(4), 5.

Vasut, R. (2016, June 30). Comparing databases: A brief look at academic search complete and periodical archive online. Retrieved from https://ryanvasut.com/2016/06/29/comparing-databases-a-brief-look-at-academic-search-complete-and-periodical-archive-online/

Wenzler, J. (2013). Keeping the enemy close: Integrating Google Scholar into the online academic library. *Against the Grain, 20*(3), 1. Retrieved from http://docs.lib.purdue.edu/cgi/viewcontent.cgi?article=2393&context=atg

Whitt, J. (2017). ACI scholarly blog index. *The Charleston Advisor, 18*(4), 5–9. Retrieved from https://doi.org/10.5260/chara.18.4.5

CHAPTER 7

Reference Managers: Saving and Storing Your Research

Chapter Learning Objectives:

- Identify and describe the top four reference managers.
- Define a reference manager.
- Discuss the reference-management life cycle.
- Discuss the importance of reference managers.
- Discuss how Microsoft Word can be used as a reference manager.
- List the basic features of a reference manager.
- Explain how Microsoft Academic integrates with Microsoft Word.

What Is a Reference Manager?

Scholarly writing is critical to the research process, and the discovery of literature, to aid in that process, is just as important. Reference managers, **bibliographic managers**, **citation managers**, or personal bibliographic file managers are all synonymous terms used to describe a software tool used to store bibliographic or citation information. In the past, manual methods were used to organize citations, which was a cumbersome, inaccurate, and time-consuming process. Saving files and copying and pasting bibliographic data within spreadsheets was not uncommon. The main purpose of reference-management software is to systematically manage, store, organize, and format references for discovered literature. It assists in constructing a database of literature and formatting references in a variety of citation styles like APA, MLA, and Chicago (Basak, 2014; Pradhan & Nayak, 2017).

bibliographic manager

A software tool used to store bibliographic information from journals, books, articles, and more.

citation manager

Also called a bibliographic manager or reference manager. Used to store bibliographic information.

THE IMPORTANCE OF REFERENCE MANAGERS

The most important reason to use a reference manager tool is to save time and improve productivity. **Reference managers** are essential to practicing good

reference manager

Also called bibliographic manager or citation manager. Used to store bibliographic information.

research and managing bibliographic content. Research is a collaborative process, and reference managers can enhance this process by sharing literature and citations. Using this collective tool increases brainstorming, communication, conversation, and information sharing, and eliminates geographic boundaries (Brody, 2017; Necka, 2013). Reference managers also combat plagiarism through citation support. Remember, "a **citation** is a way of giving credit to individuals for their creative and intellectual works that you utilized to support research" (Wiggins, 2017, para. 2). Reference managers are used to establish good scholarship. Finally, reference managers are our environmental allies in tree conservation by no longer needing to print and store paper.

REFERENCE-MANAGEMENT LIFE CYCLE

reference-management life cycle

Activities performed after the discovery of literature: create, store, organize, cite, change, and share.

The **life cycle of reference management** begins with the discovery of literature while performing searches in aggregators such as EBSCO or ProQuest. After discovering the desired literature, the basic functions of management software are enacted, which create, store, organize, change, cite, and share references (Singh, 2017) (Figure 7.1).

1. Create: Citation information is exported from database.
2. Store: Citation information is stored within the reference manager, either desktop or web based.
3. Organize: Create tags, groups, folders, annotations, web links, or full-text articles.
4. Cite: Insert citations and create reference/bibliography/works cited page within word processor.
5. Change: Switch between citation styles, such as APA, MLA, or Chicago.
6. Share: Collaborate by sharing references with other people.

FIGURE 7.1

Reference-Management Life Cycle

KEY TOOLS OF WRITING AND RESEARCH *A Guide for the Student Writer*

FEATURES OF A REFERENCE MANAGER

All reference managers have the same basic features. These key features are:

- Creating a collection of citations by building a database of literature
- Importing citations from aggregators and databases
- Formatting citations in various styles
- Saving and organizing Portable Document Formats (PDF), screenshots, graphs, and web pages
- Collecting metadata (bibliographic information) from PDF files
- Downloading abstracts and annotations of citations
- Sharing data between groups and other reference managers
- Integrating with word processors with a write-and-cite feature that facilitates in-text citations, footnotes, endnotes, or reference pages
- Cloud synchronization
- Free account creation and data-storage options
- Online help forums

metadata

Bibliographic information about books, journals, articles, magazines, or pictures. It is data about the bibliographic data.

cloud synchronization

File-backup system. Saves files from a desktop or laptop onto another company's server rather than a personal computer.

Not all reference managers will have the same features. However, you should choose the right software according to your personal computer's system settings and storage capacity (Chawla & Gupta, 2017; Parabhoi, Seth, & Pathy, 2017; Pradhan & Nayak, 2017; Singh, 2017) (Figures 7.2 and 7.3).

The Big Four

Currently, ProQuest's RefWorks, EndNote, Mendeley, and Zotero are popular reference-management software on the market today. Researchers, students, and instructors at colleges and universities all over the world use these reference managers to improve workflow in the research process.

PROQUEST REFWORKS

RefWorks (www.refworks.com) is a commercial web-based software developed in 2001 by ProQuest that requires a username and password to gain access. It is a fee-based reference manager that can be purchased by individuals. However, it is used primarily by libraries and academic institutions based on their access to the ProQuest aggregator. A popular feature of this reference manager is Write-N-Cite, an optional utility that integrates with Microsoft Word. This MS Word–RefWorks integration allows the user to immediately format research papers including in-text citations, footnotes, and a reference page (Basak, 2014).

RefWorks

A fee-based reference manager that can be purchased by individuals.

ENDNOTE

A popular fee-based reference-management software used to store bibliographic information.

EndNote (www.endnote.com) is another popular reference-management application. It is owned by Clarivate Analytics, formally known as Thomson Reuters. This is a fee-based software that can be purchased as web-based, desktop, or mobile versions. EndNote is used by individuals and academic institutions, and it touts a basic version for students who cannot afford the desktop version. The free version is a good primer for learning how to use EndNote, and then you can purchase an upgrade. A free trial is also available (Chawla & Gupta, 2017).

MENDELEY

Free reference-management software used to store bibliographic information.

Mendeley (www.mendeley.com) is free and available in desktop and web-based formats. Both versions can be synchronized to save all citations in the cloud. Mendeley has two basic strategies that give it an advantage. The first strategy involves downloading discovered literature. By dragging and dropping PDF files into the Mendeley desktop window, citation information is extracted from the PDF file. The second strategy allows Mendeley to import citations via a web browser plug-in. As with all reference managers, citation sharing is available where a citation collection can be made "public." However, this does not allow access to view PDF files. Additionally, Really Simple Syndication (RSS) feeds can be used to subscribe to public citation collections. Premium software packages are available at a reasonable price based on the personal online library storage space you need (Gilmour & Cobus-Kno, 2011; Pradhan & Nayak, 2017).

ZOTERO

Popular free reference-management software touted as a personal research assistant. Used to store bibliographic information.

Zotero (www.zotero.org)—pronounced zoh-TAIR-oh—is a free open-source citation-management software created by George Mason University's Center for History and New Media. Originally built as a plug-in for Firefox, Zotero has long since expanded to include Chrome and Safari stand-alone desktop applications. Zotero lightens the burden of the research process by allowing a one-click process that senses and saves metadata to a personally created database. The personal database is both a desktop and cloud-based application. Zotero uses translators that recognize journal articles, books, news articles, websites, and other digital objects, which provide seamless importing of academic and nonacademic records. Zotero adds PDFs, images, audio and video files, and snapshots of web pages (Coar & Sewell, 2010; Ray & Ramesh, 2017).

Content	RefWorks	EndNote	Zotero	Mendeley
Developer	ProQuest	Clarivate Analytics	Roy Rosenzweig Center for History and New Media	Mendeley Ltd.
Web-Browser Compatibility	Internet Explorer, Firefox, Safari	Internet Explorer, Firefox, Safari (online version)	Firefox, Chrome, Safari	Internet Explorer, Firefox, Safari, Chrome
Word-Processor Compatibility	MS Word for Windows/ Mac, Open Office, Rich Text Files	MS Word for Windows/ Mac, Open Office	MS Word for Windows, Open Office, Libre Office	MS Word for Windows, Open Office, Libre Office
Free Access	No	No	Yes	Yes (free versions only)
Export from Online Databases	Yes	Yes	Yes	Yes
Import from RSS Feeds	Yes	No	Yes	No
Search Online Catalogs and Databases	Yes	Yes	No	No
Share References Online	Yes	Yes	Yes	Yes
Mobile Web Version	Yes	No	No	No
Customized for Subscribing Organization	Yes	No	No	Only into institutional edition
Maximum Number of Records	Unlimited	Unlimited	Unlimited	Unlimited
Online Storage Space Limits	5 GB per account	5 GB through EndNote Web	300 MB free, additional space available on purchase	1 GB personal and 500 MB shared for free, additional space available on purchase

Note. Adapted from *Automated Reference Management: A Solution for Scholarly Communication* by B. Pradhan and S. Nayak, 2017, 73, p.189-193.

FIGURE 7.2

Reference-Management Software Comparison

FIGURE 7.3

*Other Notable Reference-
Management Software*

Cite U Like	www.citeulike.org	Free web-based reference-management software for creating, managing, and discovering sources
ReadCube	www.readcube.com	Free web-based software that allows Google Scholar searches within ReadCube. In addition, ReadCube offers article recommendation to further research efforts.
BibMe	www.bibme.org	Free web-based reference-management software for building bibliography online

Mini Managers

mini managers

Small reference managers inside software programs and databases.

Mini managers are small reference managers contained within software programs and databases. Most students and researchers do not know they exist. Mini managers are useful when writing papers that require limited references. The final benefit of mini citation managers is the allowance to learn proper citation and easily keep track of citations for smaller research papers.

PROQUEST

ProQuest has a small reference manager contained within its aggregator. As stated in Chapter 6, ProQuest allows you to create a reference page from saved research. Creating a reference page is easy—all you must do is select all of the research and click **Cite** to create a properly formatted reference page in different citation styles (Figure 7.4).

FIGURE 7.4

ProQuest Reference Manager

MICROSOFT WORD

Contained within Microsoft Word is a mini bibliographic manager. You can import bibliographic data (metadata) from Microsoft Academic, manually enter it, and create in-text citations and reference pages. On the References tab, in the Citations and Bibliography group, the Manage Sources feature allows you to add citations and import them from Microsoft Academic (Figure 7.5).

FIGURE 7.5

Importing Citations from Microsoft Academic into Microsoft Word

1.

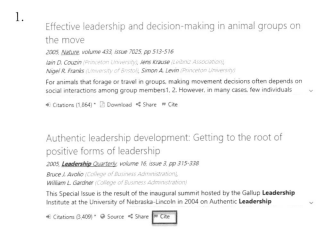

Locate information in Microsoft Academic and click **Cite** to download citation.

2.

Microsoft Academic creates a citation box with all of the cited articles. Click **Microsoft Word** to download citations.

3.

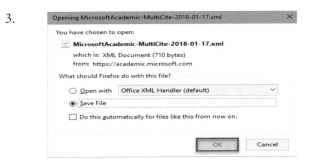

Citations can be saved to "download" onto a computer.

4.

Open Microsoft Word, click on **References** then **Manage Sources**, then click **Browse**.

5.

Go to Downloads and select file.

6.

Sources are now in Microsoft Word reference manager. Click **Copy into current list**.

All references placed in Microsoft Word can automatically generate an in-text citation and reference page. If you do not use Microsoft Academic to download references into Microsoft Word, then you must input the metadata manually. However, it would be easier to find the citation in Microsoft Academic, and then import to save time. Importing citations into Microsoft Word does not work when using Google Scholar.

Summary

Now that your research is in progress, keeping up with everything, namely the literature you found using aggregators, databases, and research portals, is a daunting task. Reference managers are critical tools in the research process because they serve as a personal research assistant, creating a database of literature for current and future use. The "Big Four" reference managers are ProQuest RefWorks, EndNote, Mendeley, and Zotero. Conversely, there are mini managers within the ProQuest aggregator and Microsoft Word. Reference managers are a critical component of creating a successful and accurate reference page.

Key Terms

Bibliographic managers

Citation manager

Cloud synchronization

EndNote

Mendeley

Metadata

Mini managers

Reference-management life cycle

Reference manager

RefWorks

Zotero

Review Questions

1. What is the importance of using reference-management software?
2. Explain the reference-management life cycle.
3. How would you apply the reference-management life cycle to your own work?
4. Describe the feature and benefits of using a reference manager.
5. What are the pros and cons of using each reference-management software application?
6. How do mini managers benefit writers?
7. Discuss Microsoft Academic and how it integrates with Microsoft Word.
8. What are the steps in using Microsoft Word as a reference manager?

References

Basak, S. K. (2014). Reference management software: Comparative analysis of RefWorks and Zotero. *World Academy of Science, Engineering and Technology, International Journal of Computer, Electrical, Automation, Control and Information Engineering*, 8(11), 1982–1985. Retrieved from http://www.waset.org/publications/9999686

Brody, S. (2017). Web-based tools for collaborative research. *Library Hi Tech News*, 34(8), 8–19. Retrieved from https://doi.org/10/gcm2vc

Chawla, V., & Gupta, M. (2017). Reference management softwares: A study of Endnote, Mendeley, Refwork, Zotero. *Kaav International Journal of Science, Engineering & Technology*, 4(3), 8–12.

Coar, J. T., & Sewell, J. P. (2010). Zotero: Harnessing the power of a personal bibliographic manager. *Nurse Educator*, 35(5), 205–207. Retrieved from https://doi.org/10.1097/NNE.0b013e3181ed81e4

Gilmour, R., & Cobus-Kno, L. (2011). Reference management software: A comparative analysis of four products. *Issues in Science and Technology Librarianship*, 66. Retrieved from https://doi.org/10.5062/F4Z60KZF

Necka, E. (2013). Selecting a reference manager. *Psychological Science Agenda*, 27(11). Retrieved from http://www.apa.org/science/about/psa/2013/12/reference-manager.aspx

Parabhoi, L., Seth, A. K., & Pathy, S. K. (2017). Citation management software tools: A comparison with special reference to Zotero and Mendeley. *Journal of Advances in Library and Information Science*, 6(3), 288–293.

Pradhan, B., & Nayak, S. (2017). Automated reference management: A solution for scholarly communication. *International Journal of Library and Information Studies*, 73(3), 189–193. Retrieved from http://ijlis.org/img/2017_vol_7_issue_3/189-193.pdf

Ray, A. K., & Ramesh, D. B. (2017). Zotero: Open source citation management tool for researchers. *International Journal of Library and Information Studies*, 7(3), 238–245.

Singh, B. P. (2017). Reference management software's (RMS): A boon to changing scholarly communication landscape. *Journal of Information Management, 4*(1), 1–13.

Wiggins, M. (2017, September 13). LibGuides: Citation styles: APA, MLA, Chicago, Turabian, IEEE: Home [Library Guide]. Retrieved from https://pitt.libguides.com/c.php?g=12108&p=64729

CHAPTER 8

Revising, Editing, and Proofreading

Chapter Learning Objectives:

- Discuss the ARRR approach.
- Define revising, editing, and proofreading.
- Explain the advantages of using checklists.
- Explain the differences between content editing, developmental editing, and mechanical editing.
- Identify software tools used for editing.

Achieving Clarity in Writing

Many professionals and students find the revising, editing, and proofreading process a daunting task. Since good writing is essential for success in school and business, the revising, editing, and proofreading process is vital for clarity, cohesiveness, credibility, and correctness. For it to work, there should be some form of organization within the work before beginning, whether it is on paper or in the mind of the writer. Examining the written word can be a difficult process, especially if the writer has been working on the project for a long period of time. After a long writing project, the writer is unable to see the mistakes within their own work, so they must take a break from the work to regain vision and clarity (Heffernan & Lincoln, 1994; McWhorter, 2016). Revising, editing, and proofreading (REP) improves your REP-utation as a serious student writer.

Revising

revising

Revising means to look again, to reexamine, rethink, straighten out, review, and reappraise a paper. All of these synonyms support what needs to happen during

To reexamine, rethink, straighten out, review, and reappraise a paper.

the revision process. Revision is taking multiple looks at your text to convey a clear message to the reader. Taking another look includes making changes, adding words, moving paragraphs, and improving ideas. Revision places emphasis on the entire paper and how all the parts are related to conveying a complete learning experience for the reader. Revision is a positive attempt to improve the strengths and eliminate the weaknesses of a writer's work (Ede, 2004). It is simple innovation because it generates growth through improvement and new insight into one's own work. Revising naturally follows the add, rearrange, remove, and replace approach (ARRR) (Solikhah, Pandawa, & Pucangan, 2017) (Figure 8.1).

FIGURE 8.1

Revising Process

Add	Increases word count and content. May need additional research to add more content and material.
Rearrange	Reorganizes the content for clarity and flow. Consider the sequencing, pace, and flow of words.
Remove	Delete content, paragraphs, and passages, or make changes.
Replace	Substitute, swap, or exchange. Ask for a second opinion and outside source to gain a fresh perspective.

checklist

Written tasks that must be performed.

FIGURE 8.2

Revising Checklist

Revising improves critical-thinking skills by evaluating the content of the text. Evaluation is essential for good revision because it allows the writer to judge the purpose, value, content, and development of the material. The best approach to revision for inexperienced academic writers is to use checklists. **Checklists** are written tasks that must be performed. They are used as a guide, learning tool, and reminder of what to look for when revising (Figure 8.2).

		Content	
❏	Confirm thesis statement. In formal academic writing, the thesis statement appears near the end of the introduction.		**Thesis**
❏	Is the focus/purpose of the paper clear?		
❏	Confirm the introduction gives a history, background, and overview of the topic.		
❏	The introduction clearly states the purpose and primary topic that will be developed within the paper.		**Introduction**
❏	Ensure the introduction prepares the reader for what follows.		

❏	Confirm that the paper clearly conveys a purpose and addresses an appropriate audience.	**Body**
❏	What additional detail, evidence, or counterarguments might strengthen the paper?	
❏	Is there any material that is irrelevant to the purpose of the paper?	
❏	Confirm explanation of important terms/concepts that are discussed in the paper.	
❏	Delete any details that do not support the main idea or thesis.	
❏	Delete any repeating ideas, themes, or statements.	
❏	Confirm that the content of the paper supports your thesis statement. Look at your outline; does it support your thesis statement or your purpose of writing the paper?	
❏	Confirm the paper has an effective conclusion.	**Conclusion**
❏	Ensure concluding paragraph restates or ties back to your thesis statement.	
	Organization and Paragraph Development	**Paragraph Development**
❏	Are the major points connected and the relationships between points explained clearly?	
❏	Are all major points related to the topic, and do they contribute to answering the question or assignments?	
❏	Each paragraph must begin with a topic sentence. Sentences must flow smoothly and logically from one to the other.	
❏	Confirm each paragraph is clear and complete; do they need more evidence and detail? A paragraph is four to six sentences.	
❏	Confirm that the paper is written in the third person, unless otherwise noted by the assignment.	
❏	Ensure the appropriate transition of words so the reader can move from one idea to the next.	
❏	Rewrite any ideas or sentences that are unclear or confusing.	**Sentence Development**
❏	Check that all sentences are written in the same verb tense (past, present, or future).	
❏	Rewrite sentences to include more powerful and vivid language.	
❏	Replace words that are used repeatedly with synonyms.	
❏	Ensure that sentences are of varied length and structure.	
❏	Ensure that ideas flow logically from one idea/point to another using good transitional words and phrases.	
❏	Confirm that paragraphs include a clear main idea or topic sentence.	
❏	Ensure that the paper has headings that support its organization. Remember, your outline can become headings.	

continued...

		Evidentiary Support	
❏	Confirm that all ideas, quotes, and sources of information are cited.		**Citations/References**
❏	Confirm the use of a consistent referencing style (APA, MLA, Chicago).		
❏	Confirm quotations are properly introduced, accurately presented, and correctly formatted.		
❏	Ensure that quotations add evidence. Would paraphrasing be more effective?		
❏	Confirm that references are at the end of the paper. The references appear right after the conclusion on a separate page within the same document.		
		Focus	
❏	Confirm all objectives of the assignment have been accomplished.		**Assignment Guidelines**
❏	Confirm the paper meets the needs, interest, and expectations of the reader.		
❏	Confirm that all questions of the assignment have been answered.		

evidentiary support

Scholarly articles to support claims made in the paper. They are fulfilled by using in-text citations.

This revising checklist is adapted from Northeastern State University Broken Arrow (2015), (2014), and Sullivan and Eggleston (2006).

Editing

Editing focuses on the nuts and bolts of the entire produced work. It allows the writer to polish the manuscript, essay, or research paper by focusing on grammar, spelling, and punctuation errors, a process that only takes place after revising has been completed. Content, development, and mechanical editing are distinct levels of editing to be used depending on the size and importance of the project. Editing involves reading closely to allow the writer to accomplish clarity, coherency, consistency, and correctness of a body of work.

content editing

Editing a body of work to ensure your words are correctly communicated to an audience. Content editing is concerned with factual accuracy and inconsistent statements within a paper.

developmental editing

Reorganizes and restructures a body of work; reviews the overall structure of the paper.

mechanical editing

Reviews spelling, grammar, punctuation, capitalization, abbreviations, and formatting of lists, headings, and tables.

CONTENT, DEVELOPMENTAL, AND MECHANICAL EDITING

Content editing involves editing a body of work to ensure its words are correctly communicated to an audience. It deals with the connection of ideas throughout the entire paper. Additionally, it is concerned with factual accuracy and inconsistent statements within a paper. A writer during this phase should verify and revise any facts that are incorrect. Developmental editing reorganizes and restructures a body of work; it reviews the overall structure of the paper. When a student rewrites sections of a paper to improve the flow and clarity, they are practicing developmental editing. Mechanical editing reviews spelling, grammar, punctuation, capitalization, abbreviations, and formatting of lists, headings, and tables, to name a few. When mechanical editing takes place, the writer is looking at the paper line by line and letter by letter to ensure consistency and correctness. Overall, the editing process pays special attention to word choices, flow, and sentence structure (Einsohn, 2011).

HOW LONG DOES EDITING TAKE?

According to Einsohn (2011), "Mechanical editing requires a sharp eye, grasp of a wide range of conventions, and good judgement" (p. 5). Editing takes time, and the length of the project will determine if a writer should apply light, medium, or heavy editing. If it is a project that will be published, then it should be heavily edited. If it is for an assignment, then apply medium editing. If it is only a couple of pages, then of course, it only needs light editing. Sullivan and Eggleston (2006) stated that for two complete readings of a medium-level project on an 8.5 × 11-in. paper, assume four to six pages per hour. Other estimates are 250 words per hour. Editing is most effective when it is performed in allotted time increments. Do not attempt to write and edit in the same day. Edit for a couple of hours, then get up and walk away to refresh your mind. After a while, a writer no longer sees the mistakes in their work, so take a break and refresh your mind (Figure 8.3).

FIGURE 8.3

Editing Checklist

		Editing	
	❑	Check for incomplete sentences.	**Grammar**
	❑	Avoid run-on sentences.	
	❑	Ensure all subjects and verbs agree.	
	❑	Check that pronouns and their antecedents agree.	
	❑	Ensure correct voice according to assignment (first person, second person, or third person).	
	❑	Avoid sexist language and use gender-neutral language.	
	❑	Keep consistent verb tense throughout the essay.	
	❑	Ensure sentences contain appropriate end punctuation.	**Punctuation and Mechanics**
	❑	Use commas correctly.	
	❑	Use semicolons, colons, and dashes effectively and correctly.	
	❑	Use quotations marks correctly.	
	❑	Ensure the first word of each sentence is capitalized.	
	❑	Ensure proper nouns are capitalized.	
	❑	Follow rules for underlining, abbreviating, and using numbers.	
	❑	Ensure italics and boldface types are used correctly.	

continued...

❏	Avoid contractions.	**Words and Word Choices**
❏	Perform spell-check for common errors.	
❏	Avoid unnecessary, filler, or "dead" words.	
❏	Avoid using slang, "text talk," or clichés.	
❏	Ensure word choice is correct.	
❏	Does the paper require a table of contents?	**Assignment Guidelines**
❏	Ensure paper follows guidelines, instructions, or grade rubric for the course.	

Note. Editing checklist is adapted from Northeastern State University Broken Arrow (2015) and Sullivan and Eggleston (2006).

Proofreading

proofreading

The final check for errors in a document.

Proofreading is the final check for errors in a document. When proofreading, the writer is searching for minor errors missed in the revising and editing phase. Proofreading is the polish that allows the paper to shine; it is the final check for accuracy before the document is released to be graded by the instructor (Carduner, 2007; Einsohn, 2011; Marchisan & Alber, 2001). Please remember that proofreading is not a one-time occurrence, the process of proofreading is repeated over and over again until the document is accurate and error-free (Anderson, 2006; Sullivan & Eggleston, 2006). In essence, proofreading is about verifying the document's accuracy (Pagel & Norstrom, 2011). Proofreading is not skimming the document; it requires skill, patience, knowledge, and attention to detail to unearth errors (Pagel & Norstrom, 2011). Proofreading is best performed with a checklist. However, before beginning the proofreading process, walk away from the document to give your brain a chance to reset and reboot. After living with a document for several weeks, sometimes it is difficult to see the errors (Figure 8.4).

No software program can revise a person's creative work. Revising is an individual or group process of changing a document to create clarity, unification, and coherence. Microsoft Word's Track Changes is an excellent tool for editing, reviewing, and group collaboration. It allows for comments and records when and where changes are made to the document. The author of the document can accept or reject changes made by an editor or group.

However, editing and proofreading can be made easier using software programs and integrated application (Figure 8.5). For example, students and editors use applications such as Microsoft Word's spelling and grammar checker to ensure the accuracy of their work.

FIGURE 8.4

Proofreading Checklist

	Basic Proofreading Checklist	
❏	Ensure directions were followed. Check syllabus or grade rubric for directions.	**Assignment Directions**
❏	Confirm the minimum word count of the assignment and ensure the paper meets it without exceeding the maximum word count. Check syllabus or grade rubric for confirmation.	
❏	Confirm that the title page, paper setup, and page numbering are consistent with APA guidelines.	**APA Formatting Requirements**
❏	Ensure margins are uniform. One-inch margins are required at the top, bottom, left, and right of the page.	
❏	Confirm that the paper uses Times New Roman, Arial, or Courier font.	
❏	Confirm that the paper uses 12-point font.	
❏	Confirm that paragraphs are indented half an inch, five spaces, or one full tab.	
❏	Confirm the title page, body text, and reference page are double spaced.	
❏	Confirm the omission of first- and second-person writing. Only write in the third person.	**Paragraphs, Headings, and Writing Mechanics**
❏	Confirm the abstract is between 150 and 250 words. The abstract appears before the introduction.	
❏	Confirm the word "Introduction" does not appear before the introductory paragraph. Replace the word "Introduction" with the title of your paper.	
❏	Confirm the heading levels are in alignment with the organization of the paper.	
❏	Confirm avoidance of one-sentence paragraphs or paragraphs that are too long. Paragraphs should be between four to six sentences.	
❏	Confirm avoidance of contractions, slang, and abbreviations.	
❏	Confirm elimination of words that are vague, filler, or redundant.	
❏	Perform a final spelling, grammar, and punctuation check.	
❏	Confirm in-text citations for summaries, paraphrases, and direct quotations.	**Crediting Sources**
❏	Confirm that every in-text citation has a matching reference in the reference page.	
❏	Confirm that websites are properly cited.	
❏	Read paper aloud for final error check.	**Final Check**

Note. Proofreading checklist is adapted from Northeastern State University Broken Arrow (2015) and Sullivan and Eggleston (2006).

FIGURE 8.5

Other Software Tools for Editing and Proofreading

Name	Website	Plug-ins	Cost
Grammarly	www.grammarly.com	MS Word plug-in; Firefox, Chrome, Edge plug-in	Free for basic spelling and grammar; cost for premium access
Ginger	www.gingersoftware.com	Windows integration; Chrome and Safari plug-in	Free for basic spelling and grammar; cost for premium access
Style Writer 4	www.editorsoftware.com	Software program for editing and proofreading	Cost for software
WordRake	www.wordrake.com	MS Word and Outlook Integration; also available for Mac	Cost for software

REAP

Revising, editing, accuracy, and proofreading.

Remember, Revising and Editing create Accuracy in a document; Proofreading is the polishing before submitting (**REAP**). Here are checkpoints for the REAP process:

1. Read paper aloud for revisions.
2. Edit using your word processor's spelling and grammar check to find and correct errors.
3. Use software applications such as Grammarly, Ginger, or WordRake for editing and proofreading to increase accuracy.
4. Have a second or third person read the document.

Summary

To reap the rewards of a good paper, a student writer must revise, edit, and proofread to create accuracy, cohesion, and readability within a document. Revising, editing, and proofreading are best performed by using checklists. Checklists ensure the writer stays on track. Additionally, checklists are a tool for learning how and what to revise, edit, and proofread. Software applications such as Grammarly can assist in editing and proofreading; however, no software application can revise. Revision lies within the heart and mind of the writer.

Key Terms

Checklist
Content editing
Developmental editing
Evidentiary support

Mechanical editing
Proofreading
REAP
Revising

Review Questions

1. Discuss the importance of checklists during the editing and proofreading process.
2. How does the ARRR approach apply in revising an essay or research paper?
3. What is the difference between content editing, mechanical editing, and developmental editing?
4. If you had a 1,500-word essay, how long would it take to edit?
5. Explain the difference between revising, editing, and proofreading.
6. Identify and describe the REAP process.

References

Anderson, L. K. (2006). *McGraw-Hill's proofreading handbook* (2nd ed.). New York, NY: McGraw-Hill Education.

Carduner, J. (2007). Teaching proofreading skills as a means of reducing composition errors. *Language Learning Journal, 35*(2), 283–295. Retrieved from https://doi.org/10.1080/09571730701317655

Ede, L. (2004). *Work in progress: A guide to academic writing and revising* (6th ed.). Boston, MA: Bedford/St. Martin's.

Einsohn, A. (2011). *The copyeditor's handbook: A guide for book publishing and corporate communications* (3rd ed.). Berkeley, CA: University of California Press.

Heffernan, J. A. W., & Lincoln, J. E. (1994). *Writing: A college handbook* (4th ed.). New York, NY: W. W. Norton & Co Inc.

Marchisan, M. L., & Alber, S. R. (2001). The write way: Tips for teaching the writing process to resistant writers. *Intervention in School and Clinic, 36*(3), 154–162. Retrieved from https://doi.org/10.1177/105345120103600304

McWhorter, K. T. (2016). *Successful college writing with 2016 MLA update* (6th ed.). Boston, MA: Bedford/St. Martin's.

Northeastern State University Broken Arrow. (2015). *The writer's toolkit.* Retrieved from https://academics.nsuok.edu/Portals/24/Revising%20and%20Editing%20Checklist.pdf.

Pagel, L., & Norstrom, B. (2011). *Proofreading and editing precision* (6th ed.). Mason, OH: Cengage Learning.

Solikhah, I., Pandawa, J. I., & Pucangan, K. (2017). Drafting and revising strategies to develop english essay by EFL Indonesian learners. *IJOLTL: Indonesian Journal of Language Teaching and Linguistics, 5*(13), 919–930. Retrieved from https://doi.org/10.21474/IJAR01/3591

Sullivan, K. D., & Eggleston, M. (2006). *The McGraw-Hill desk reference for editors, writers, and proofreaders* (1st ed.). New York, NY: McGraw-Hill Education.

CHAPTER 9

Plagiarism

Chapter Learning Objectives:

- Define plagiarism.
- Discuss the types of plagiarism.
- Discuss the categories of plagiarism.
- Identify examples of plagiarism.
- Discuss the causes of plagiarism.
- Discuss the punishment for plagiarism.
- Discuss student's responsibility concerning plagiarism.
- Identify and list the tools for plagiarism.

Our world is created by thought, speech, and the written word. It is the thought that is real; the physical world is a manifestation of thought. The written word is our hidden thoughts coming to life for everyone to read, digest, and to change the lives and destinies of people. When our words are kidnapped, it is a mental, physical, and ethical violation. Academic integrity, copyrights, patents, and trademarks are the protection of creative thought that has come to life.

What Is Plagiarism?

Plagiarism is defined as intellectual theft of text, data, PowerPoints, spreadsheets, knowledge, or ideas (Shashok, 2011; Smith, 2016). It is considered cheating because the person who is plagiarizing is not using original thought. It surfaces as a moral issue in society that most people are aware of but do not consider a serious issue except in academic, publishing, and entertainment industries. Plagiarism equates to theft, and it does not matter whether the work is published or unpublished—the fact that someone else's words were used without giving

academic integrity

Moral and ethical code that states cheating will be avoided.

copyright

Owner-exclusive right to creative works such as books, journal articles, music, and more.

patent

Sole rights to an invention that was approved by the government for a limited period of time.

trademark

A symbol, word, or design that is registered with the pto.gov as a unique expression of that organization. Logos are an example of designs that can be trademarked.

plagiarism

Intellectual theft of text, data, PowerPoints, spreadsheets, knowledge, or ideas.

intellectual property

Creative works such as books, movies, and articles that are owned by a person, group, or organization.

copyright infringement

Occurs when a copyrighted work is reproduced, distributed, performed, publicly displayed, or made into a derivative (preexisting) work without the permission of the copyright owner.

proper credit is a violation of the writer's **intellectual property** (Akbar, 2018). When a student plagiarizes, misrepresentation occurs because the plagiarist allows the reader to think the work is their original thoughts, words, or creativity. Finally, plagiarism is a violation of United States copyright laws. The law states: "**Copyright infringement** occurs when a copyrighted work is reproduced, distributed, performed, publicly displayed, or made into a derivative [preexisting] work without the permission of the copyright owner" (Dhammi & Ul Haq, 2016; US Copyright Office, n.d.). Students and researchers are well aware that plagiarism is unethical behavior. Yet, the actions of literacy theft continue to thrive, whether intentional or unintentional.

Types of Plagiarism

UNINTENTIONAL PLAGIARISM

unintentional plagiarism

Plagiarism occurs accidently; it is perceived as innocent plagiarism that occurs due to a lack of writing skill and knowledge.

Plagiarism will always be considered cheating. However, to determine the type of plagiarism, one must look at intent. When looking at intent, plagiarism falls into two main categories: unintentional and intentional (Figure 9.1). **Unintentional plagiarism** occurs accidentally; it is perceived as innocent plagiarism that results from a lack of writing skill and knowledge. In other words, the writer's inability to properly summarize, paraphrase, and cite sources causes unintentional plagiarism. Although the intent is not to plagiarize, it is still considered plagiarism (Shah, 2018; Walker, 2008). Writing is a skill that must be developed over time. Walker (2008) and Roig (1999) believe that unintentional plagiarism occurs because students do not understand plagiarism, its meaning, or its consequences.

INTENTIONAL PLAGIARISM

intentional plagiarism

Direct plagiarism is blatant cheating.

self-plagiarism

Using one's own work as new and original.

Intentional or direct plagiarism is blatant cheating. The writer copies text word for word from the original author's work. Intentional plagiarism is a deliberate and dishonest act; it is a judgment call. The writer makes the decision to deceive and mislead the reader. The motive is to commit fraud and theft for the sake of completing an assignment. Intentional plagiarism comes in different forms, such as self-plagiarism. **Self-plagiarism** is intentional plagiarism because the author is submitting work as new work, when instead it is rehashing something that has been previously written. For example, submitting the same paper in different classes for a similar assignment is self-plagiarism (Ankarali, 2018; Shah, 2018).

FIGURE 9.1

Name	Also Known As	Meaning
Direct	Cloning, Literal, or Intelligent	Exact duplication of text or data. Copying text word for word from another person's work.
Mosaic	Find-Replace or Patchworking	Borrowing from sources without using quotation marks. Neglecting to find alternative words or paraphrase.
Potluck	Remix	Copying the phrases from various sources and making all sentences fit together without using citations or quotations while keeping to the original phrasing (Myers, 2018).
Self	Recycling	Using one's own work as new and original. Submitting the same paper or parts of a paper for different assignments.
Fictitious	404 Error	Using citations that do not exist or are inaccurate (Shashok, 2011; Turnitin, 2012).
Accidental		Forgetting to cite sources, not paraphrasing properly, or misquoting.

Categories of Plagiarism

EXAMPLES OF PLAGIARISM

Chowdhury and Bhattacharyya (2018) and Smith (2016) cited several examples of plagiarism:

- Copying material without quotes, in-text citations, and/or referencing
- Paraphrasing content without in-text citation and/or referencing
- Copying ideas, words, answers, exams, or shared work from others when individual work is required
- Using another's paper in whole or in part
- Allowing another student to use one's work
- Claiming someone else's work is one's own
- Resubmitting one's own coursework when original work is required (self-plagiarism)
- Falsifying references or bibliographies
- Purchasing content and using as your own work

CAUSES OF PLAGIARISM

Earlier in this chapter, several causes of plagiarism were identified. The root causes of plagiarism are Time, Interest, Knowledge, and Access (TIKA) (Figure 9.2).

FIGURE 9.2

Causes of Plagiarism: TIKA

Time	Interest	Knowledge	Access
Waiting until the last minute to complete assignment, therefore running out of time	Lack of interest in topic or assignment	Lack of knowledge about citation and crediting sources	Easy to copy material from the Internet
Pressure to complete deadlines	Lack of motivation	Lack of knowledge about summarizing, paraphrasing, and quoting	Paper, blogs, and articles on the Internet are tempting fruit. This is known as cyber plagiarism or cyber cheating (Ankarali, 2018; Doro, 2014).
Easier to collaborate on assignments to save time		Unclear about the directions of the assignment	
Poor planning		Poor writing skills	
		Unclear definition about plagiarism, its meaning, and its consequences	
		Inexperienced researcher	

Punishment for Plagiarism

In an academic setting, plagiarism is a punishable offense by the institution, not by a court of law (Dhammi & Ul Haq, 2016). Each college and university has its own policies about plagiarism. Plagiarism violates the student code of conduct, so no student wants to be caught plagiarizing. Again, each academic institution has its own plagiarism policy. Please look at the student handbook or your institution's website for its plagiarism policy. If a student is caught plagiarizing, then the following procedure can occur:

1. The paper is reviewed by the instructor, and the type and degree of plagiarism is identified.
2. If the plagiarism is unintentional, then the instructor can have the student correct the paper and resubmit. The instructor makes the decision.

3. If intentional plagiarism is identified, then the conversation takes on a different tone. The instructor can perform the following acts:
   a. Have the student rewrite the entire assignment and resubmit for a lesser grade.
   b. Issue a grade of zero on the assignment.
   c. Issue a grade of zero on the assignment and report to the college as an academic violation, providing the entire assignment to the college, including the plagiarized sections.
4. If found guilty of several offences of plagiarism, the following can occur:
   a. A cease-and-desist letter will be sent to the student for the first offense.
   b. The student may have to repeat course.
   c. The student may be expelled from the college or university.

Prevention of Plagiarism

Plagiarism is a preventable act. You can start by learning how to credit sources—always give credit where credit is due (Foster, 2007). In academic writing, there are only three reasons to credit or cite sources, and that is when a writer is summarizing, paraphrasing, or quoting. **Summarizing** means taking ideas from a large passage and placing the main points into your own words. **Paraphrasing** uses material from another source and converts it into the your own words. It is an integration of thoughts and ideas into an essay or research paper (Wicker, 2007). **Quoting** means repeating another source word for word using quotation marks. When summarizing, paraphrasing, or quoting, in-text citations must be used because in each instance, the original thought came from someone else. In-text citation provides evidence for your work and gives credit where credit is due; it also means a reference list must be compiled (Elander, Pittam, Lusher, Fox, & Payne, 2010).

summarizing

Taking ideas from a large passage of one source and placing the main points into your own words.

paraphrasing

Converts the material from one source into the writer's own words.

quoting

Repeating another source word for word using quotation marks.

Good research is necessary to prevent plagiarism. Use scholarly research articles contained in aggregators like ProQuest, EBSCO, or Google Scholar. Limit the use of Internet sources. The Internet is a great tool for research, but blogs and commercial websites are not considered reliable sources to provide evidentiary support. If your website or blog does not contain reliable research sources, then it should not be used. Another reason to avoid random websites is the higher incidences of plagiarism when using plagiarism checkers. Inexperienced Internet researchers tend to use the same websites for research and use the same words. Plagiarism software checks websites first.

TOOLS TO PREVENT PLAGIARISM

"A writer or a researcher can get rid of plagiarism if they patiently try to check the originality of the paper they write by using plagiarism checker software that could be accessed freely on the internet" (Wajdi, Sumartana, & Hudiananingsih,

2018, p. 95). Using a plagiarism tool allows students to improve writing and paraphrasing skills, all the while learning how to avoid plagiarism. However, the use of plagiarism tools is a self-regulating and self-editing process where the student must check their own work. Plagiarism tools act as a source of prevention or intervention, detecting similarity and allowing the student to correct issues before submitting the final assignment (Kunschak, 2018; Madray, 2007) (Figure 9.3).

Most academic institutions have a subscription web-based plagiarism-software tool. The student submits a paper, then the plagiarism software compares the student's paper against (1) papers already submitted from previous students, (2) Internet sources and websites, and (3) databases housing journals, magazines, and other publications. Once the software checks or text-matches the submitted paper, it assigns a score and highlights any sections of the student's paper that are similar to other works found in the database, on the Internet, or from other students' work. At this point, it is up to the student to correct the sections of their work that have the highest similarity score (Chowdhury & Bhattacharyya, 2018; Heckler, Rice, & Bryan, 2013).

| FIGURE 9.3

Leading Plagiarism Checkers | | |

Plagiarism Tool	Website	Comments
Turnitin	www.turnitin.com	Offered by an academic institution
SafeAssign	www.blackboard.com/safeassign/index.html	Owned by the learning-management system Blackboard
Ithenticate	www.ithenticate.com/	Owned by Plagiarism.org (Turnitin.com); used in the publishing industry

Student Responsibility

1. Start working on your paper early. Do not wait until the last minute.
2. Conduct good research. Use library aggregators and databases to perform research rather than solely depend on Internet sources.
3. Always write an annotated outline with references for every major topic. By doing this, you ensure that your evidentiary support is covered.
4. Summarize, paraphrase, or quote. However, do not overquote in your paper.
5. If there is a problem with plagiarism, then use paraphrasing tools to assist in taking a section of text and placing the information into your own words. This will then be considered original content (Figure 9.4).

FIGURE 9.4

Online Paraphrasing Tools

Paraphrasing Tool Name	Website
Spinbot	www.spinbot.com
ezArticleLink.com Free Article Spinner Online	www.ezarticlelink.com/articlespinner/free.php
Free Article Spinning Tool	www.freearticlespinning.com

6. Use plagiarism-checking software before submitting the assignment.
7. Become familiar with your college's or local library's research databases.

Summary

Plagiarism is intellectual theft of text, data, knowledge, or ideas. It falls into two main types: intentional and unintentional; both types of plagiarism are a violation of student and academic codes of conduct in most colleges. Tools such as Turnitin and SafeAssign are used to detect plagiarism. To completely prevent plagiarism, the student must learn how to summarize, paraphrase, quote, and cite material that comes from an outside source.

Key Terms

Academic integrity
Copyright
Copyright infringement
Intellectual property
Intentional plagiarism

Paraphrasing
Patent
Plagiarism
Quoting
Self-plagiarism

Summarizing
Trademark
Unintentional plagiarism

Review Questions

1. What is plagiarism, and how does it relate to theft?
2. What are the differences between intentional and unintentional plagiarism?
3. List and describe the categories of plagiarism. Give example of each category.
4. What are the causes of plagiarism? Identify any categories you fall into as a writer.
5. List the possible punishment for plagiarism.
6. Explain in detail how plagiarism is preventable.
7. What is the student's responsibility for preventing plagiarism?
8. Identify and discuss the tools for plagiarism.
9. How do you rid your work of plagiarism?
10. Identify the software applications used to prevent plagiarism.

References

Akbar, A. (2018). Defining plagiarism: A literature review. *Ethical Lingua: Journal of Language Teaching and Literature*, 5(1), 31–38. Retrieved from https://doi.org/10.30605/ethicallingua.v5i1.750

Ankarali, H. (2018). How can be avoided plagiarism in original research articles? *International Journal of Human and Health Sciences (IJHHS)*, 2(2), 47–48. Retrieved from http://dx.doi.org/10.31344/ijhhs.v2i2.25

Chowdhury, H. A., & Bhattacharyya, D. K. (2018). Plagiarism: Taxonomy, tools and detection techniques. *ArXiv Preprint ArXiv:1801.06323*. Retrieved from https://arxiv.org/abs/1801.06323v1

Dhammi, I., & Ul Haq, R. (2016). What is plagiarism and how to avoid it? *Indian Journal of Orthopaedics*; New Delhi, 50(6), 581–583. https://doi.org/10.4103/0019-5413.193485

Doró, K. (2014). Why Do Students Plagiarize? EFL Undergraduates' Views on the Reasons Behind Plagiarism. *Romanian Journal of English Studies*, 11(1), 255–263. https://doi.org/10.2478/rjes-2014-0029

Elander, J., Pittam, G., Lusher, J., Fox, P., & Payne, N. (2010). Evaluation of an intervention to help students avoid unintentional plagiarism by improving their authorial identity. *Assessment & Evaluation in Higher Education*, 35(2), 157–171. Retrieved from https://doi.org/10.1080/02602930802687745

Foster, R. L. (2007). Avoiding unintentional plagiarism. *Journal for Specialists in Pediatric Nursing*; Hoboken, 12(1), 1–2. Retrieved from https://doi.org/10.1111/j.1744-6155.2008.00127.x

Heckler, N. C., Rice, M., & Bryan, C. H. (2013). Turnitin systems: A deterrent to plagiarism in college classrooms. *Journal of Research on Technology in Education*; Eugene, 45(3), 229–248. Retrieved from https://doi.org/10.1080/15391523.2013.10782604

Kunschak, C. (2018). Multiple uses of anti-plagiarism software. *The Asian Journal of Applied Linguistics*, 5(1), 60–69. Retrieved from http://caes.hku.hk/ajal

Madray, A. (2007). Turnitin.com. *The Charleston Advisor*, 8(4), 49–52.

Myers, C. S. (2018). Plagiarism and copyright: Best practices for classroom education. *College & Undergraduate Libraries*, 25(1), 91–99. Retrieved from https://doi.org/10.1080/10691316.2017.1391028

Roig, M. (1999). When college students' attempts at paraphrasing become instances of potential plagiarism. *Psychological Reports*, 84(3), 973–982. Retrieved from https://doi.org/10.2466/pr0.1999.84.3.973

Shah, I. P. (2018). Plagiarism . . . How to prevent it. *Aayushi International Interdisciplinary Research Journal*, 5(1), 20–23.

Shashok, K. (2011). Authors, editors, and the signs, symptoms and causes of plagiarism. *Saudi Journal of Anaesthesia; Riyadh*, 5(3), 303–307. Retrieved from https://doi.org/10.4103/1658-354X.84107

Smith, L. S. (2016). Conquering plagiarism in nursing education: *Nursing*, 46(7), 17–19. Retrieved from https://doi.org/10.1097/01.NURSE.0000484035.47822.3a

Turnitin . (2012). Results : Plagiarism spectrum. Retrieved from http://turnitin.com/assets/en_us/media/plagiarism_spectrum.php

United States Copyright Office. (n.d.). Definitions (FAQ) | US Copyright Office [Web page]. Retrieved from https://www.copyright.gov/help/faq/faq-definitions.html

Wajdi, M., Sumartana, I. M., & Hudiananingsih, N. P. D. (2018). Avoiding plagiarism in writing a research paper. *Soshum: Jurnal Sosial Dan Humaniora*, 8(1), 94–102. Retrieved from http://ojs.pnb.ac.id/index.php/SOSHUM/article/view/769

Walker, A. L. (2008). Preventing unintentional plagiarism: A method for strengthening paraphrasing skills. *Journal of Instructional Psychology; Mobile*, 35(4), 387–395.

Wicker, P. (2007). Plagiarism: understanding and management. *The Journal of Perioperative Practice; Harrogate*, 17(8), 372, 377–382. Retrieved from https://doi.org/10.1177/175045890701700802

CHAPTER 10

Bringing It All Together

Chapter Learning Objectives:

- Summarize the MEAL plan and how it is used in developing paragraphs.
- Explain how transitions are used when writing an essay or research paper.
- Discuss the advantages of using a rubric.
- Explain the two types of rubrics that instructors use.
- Identify the steps in drafting an essay or research paper.

Drafting

Drafting is creating a preliminary or first version of an essay or research paper. Usually, the first round of writing contains errors, so it is considered a rough piece of work. We use the phrase "rough draft" because the expression of thought is not complete. The text that is produced is unpolished and ragged. The rough draft gives the writer a chance to put together thoughts and ideas. Additionally, a rough draft comprises an introduction, body, conclusion, in-text citations, and references. The body of the work is filled in by writing main ideas with supporting evidence to support the thesis statement (Solikhah, Pandawa, & Pucangan, 2017). There are four main tools that are extremely helpful in writing an academic paper. The first is the outline, the second is the MEAL plan, the third is a list of transition words, and the fourth is a rubric.

OUTLINE

The outline is essential because it illustrates how a writer connects ideas. The outline can become the headings in a paper, which create organization, keep the writer on track, and guide the reader through the paper. The outline also supports the thesis, which is the purpose of why the paper is being written. Once the headings are in place, the writer can begin drafting underneath each topic of the outline. Outlining is the strategy; the actual writing is the implementation. The best tool for drafting a paper is an outline because it improves the quality of the paper and reduces attention overload (Kellogg, 1988).

MEAL

MEAL plan

Elements of a paragraph: Main idea, Evidence, Analysis, and Linking.

The second essential tool is the **MEAL plan**. MEAL stands for main idea, evidence, analysis, and linking (Figure 10.1). Basically, there are four sentences to a paragraph. The main idea should be the first sentence, presenting research (evidence) is the second, the analysis of the evidence is the third, and a linking or concluding statement is the fourth. The MEAL plan allows the writer to stay focused and the writing to become more clear and concise (Capella University, 2006, 2014).

FIGURE 10.1

MEAL Plan

Main Idea	The main idea is the topic sentence. Every paragraph should start off with one that states the main point of the paragraph.
Evidence or Examples	The evidence is the research articles you find in ProQuest, EBSCO, or Google Scholar. The evidence supports the main idea.
Analysis	Analysis is the heart of a paragraph. The analysis is how the writer interprets the evidence or example.
Linking, Concluding, or Transitioning	The concluding sentence illustrates how the paragraph fits together or transitions to the next paragraph.

TRANSITION WORDS

transition words

Words that are used to connect ideas.

The third tool is a list of **transition words**. Transition words and phrases are useful to connect ideas. When a writer wants to move the reader from one concept to the next, then they use transitions based on the rhetorical mode. Misusing or leaving out transitions in writing can impede the reader's comprehension (Figure 10.2).

"A single paragraph could utilize several rhetorical strategies to accomplish its purpose. For instance, if the purpose of a paragraph is to present two ideas or subjects for comparison and contrast, then several transitions need to be carefully selected for readers to clearly understand this intention. Therefore, a series of transitions would be selected (a) to introduce the first idea (e.g., *To illustrate*), (b) to introduce the second idea for comparison (e.g., *Similarly*), (c) to choose a transition or transitions to contrast the two ideas (e.g., *While, However, On the*

KEY TOOLS OF WRITING AND RESEARCH *A Guide for the Student Writer*

other hand, Yet), and finally (d) to choose a transition to concede a point about (e.g., *Granted*) or to conclude something about the two ideas (e.g., *Consequently*)" (Capella University, 2009, para. 4).

FIGURE 10.2

Transition Words

To Introduce an Example		
As a case in point	As an illustration	As such
For example	For instance	In general
In particular	Specifically	To illustrate

To Add Another Point, Qualification, or Idea		
Actually	Additionally	Again
Also	As proof	Besides
Equally important	Finally	First
For the most part	Further	Furthermore
In addition	In fact	Incidentally
Indeed	Lastly	Likewise
Moreover	Perhaps	Probably
Second	Secondly	What's more

To Emphasize or Clarify		
Above all	As a matter of fact	Especially
In fact	In other words	In this case
Indeed	Most importantly	Obviously
Put another way	Surely	That is
That is to say	Under certain circumstances	Undoubtedly
Up to a point	Without a doubt	

To Indicate Cause and Effect		
Accordingly	As a consequence	As a result
Consequently	Due to	For this reason
Hence	Indeed	Subsequently
Therefore	Thus	

To Intensify		
By all means	Certainly	Undoubtedly
In fact	Indeed	More important
Moreover	No	Of course
Surely	To be sure	To repeat
To tell the truth	Without doubt	Yes

continued...

To Concede a Point		
Certainly	Granted	Naturally
No doubt	Of course	Surely

To Express or Move through Time		
After/afterward	As soon as	At last
At length	At present	At the same time
Briefly	Currently	During
Eventually	Finally	First, Second, Third
Following	Immediately	In the meantime
Later	Meanwhile	Next
Now	Once	Sometimes
Soon	Still	Subsequently
Then	Until	When/Whenever

To Express Illustration		
Another example	As an illustration	Case in point
For example	For instance	In particular
One example	Specifically	To illustrate

To Compare		
Also	Both	But also
In a similar fashion	In the same manner	In the same way
Like	Likewise	Not only
One similarity	Similarly	Since

To Contrast		
Although	Although this is true	Another difference
At the same time	Conversely	However
In contrast	Meanwhile	Nevertheless
Nonetheless	Notwithstanding	On the contrary
On the other hand	One difference	Otherwise
Though	Unlike	Whereas
While this is true	Yet	

To Emphasize Effects, Consequences, or Results		
Again	As a result	Because of this
Before	Consequently	Especially
Finally	For this reason	In fact
Next	Now	Then
Therefore	Thus	To begin
To emphasize	To repeat	Under these circumstances

To Conclude or Summarize		
Accordingly	All in all	As a result
As mentioned	Consequently	Finally
Hence	In conclusion	In other words
In short	In summary	In summation
On the whole	Overall	Therefore
Thus	To conclude	To sum up
Lastly	In brief	

To Deduct		
In other words	In that case	Otherwise
Then	This implies that	

To Restate		
As has been noted	As previously stated	Given these points
In essence	In other words	In short
To put it differently		

To Generalize		
As a rule	For the most part	Generally
Generally speaking	Ordinarily	Usually

RUBRICS

The fourth helpful tool for drafting is a **rubric**, often called the grade rubric. A rubric is a grading guide that breaks down the instructions of the assignment and places point values on each section required. Many students find rubrics helpful in the writing process because they are used as a guide to ensure all topics are discussed in the assignment. Rubrics:

rubric

Grading guide that breaks down the instructions of the assignment and places point values on each section required.

- Allow students to evaluate their own work
- Improve quality of work and increase motivation

holistic rubric

Reviews the quality, proficiency, and understanding of the overall work of the student. Used to give summary feedback.

analytic rubric

A quantitative element that assigns a score to each section of the rubric. Used for more precise feedback.

- Clarify assignment expectations
- Allow for advance preparation of assignment to meet stated goals
- Promote fairness in grading

Two types of rubrics are used in the academic environment: holistic and analytic. The main purpose of a **holistic rubric** is to review the quality, proficiency, and understanding of the student's overall work (Figure 10.3). They are primarily used to give summary feedback. An **analytic rubric** adds a quantitative element by having a score assigned to each section (Figure 10.4). They are usually used for formal and more precise feedback (Gezie, Khaja, Chang, Adamek, & Johnsen, 2012; Manzanares, Baez, Ortega-Lopez, & Manso Villalain, 2015; University of New Brunswick, n.d.).

FIGURE 10.3

Sample Holistic Rubric

4	Paper demonstrates well-developed understanding of the assigned objectives. The argument is clearly developed with sufficient justification of claims. Writing is also error-free without ambiguity, and reads smoothly, creatively, and with a purpose.
3	Paper demonstrates considerable understanding of the assigned objectives. The argument is developed with some justification of claims, but may be weak in presentation and balance in developing points. Writing has some errors and ambiguities, yet does read clearly and coherently.
2	Paper demonstrates some general understanding of the assigned objectives. The argument is minimally developed with lack of justification of claims. Writing has many errors and ambiguities, and may read confusingly and incoherently.
1	Paper demonstrates understanding of the assigned objectives. The argument lacks development and does not include justification of claims. Writing also has numerous errors and reads confusingly and incoherently.

FIGURE 10.4

Sample Analytic Rubric

Criteria	Unsatisfactory	Progressing	Satisfactory	Good	Excellent
	0%	25%	50%	75%	100%
Content (100% or 100 points)	Content includes little or none of the assignment criteria.	Assignment content omits some required criteria.	Most of the required assignment content is present.	All of the required assignment content is present.	All of the required assignment content is present.

Instructions for Drafting an Essay or Research Paper

Many students find it difficult to begin drafting or start writing a paper. Writing is a process, and it can be very mechanical. The creativity comes though the expression and the analysis of research, thoughts, and ideas. The key is having a strategy, which will come in the form of your outline and research. Once the outline and research have been completed, it is a matter of filling in a template.

FIGURE 10.5

Step-by-Step Instructions for Drafting an Essay or Research Paper

Step	Instruction	Chapter		Step	Instructions	Chapter
1.	Are there instructions or a grade rubric for the assignment?	1, 10		11.	Once the first draft is completed, then read over the assignment to begin the revising and editing processes.	8
2.	If yes, break down instructions into an outline.	3		12.	Check the spelling and grammar of the assignment.	8
3.	If no, then use brainstorming techniques to build an outline.	2		13.	Ensure the paper meets the writing guidelines set forth in the rubric (APA, MLA, or Chicago).	8
4.	Research each category within your outline.	5, 6, 7		14.	Revise and edit as necessary.	8
5.	Create an annotated outline based on your research.	4, 5		15.	Check for plagiarism.	9
6.	Convert categories from your annotated outline into headings in your paper.	4		16.	Does the assignment require a PowerPoint?	3
7.	Headings are now the template for your paper.	3		17.	If yes, then transfer headings in outline over to PowerPoint. Use content from your paper to fill in the PowerPoint.	3
8.	The references are now placed in the reference page in alphabetical order.	3, 7		18.	If no, then the assignment is completed.	
9.	Now the paper has organization and paragraphs underneath each heading with a reference page.	3, 4		19.	Submit assignment	
10.	Use research to write underneath each heading using the MEAL plan.	10				

If the above steps are completed, then it should yield the student writer a passing grade for the assignment. The above steps are dependent on good research.

Summary

Compiling a paper is easy once all the other instructions in this book are followed. Crafting a paper includes four main components:

1. Outline
2. MEAL plan
3. Transition words
4. Rubric

Figure 10.5 gives systematic instructions and the chapter associated with each step in the drafting and finalizing of an essay or research paper.

Key Terms

Analytic rubric

Holistic rubric

MEAL plan

Rubric

Transition words

Review Questions

1. Summarize the MEAL plan and explain how it is used in paragraph development.
2. What are the four main tools used in drafting a paper? Describe each tool.
3. When are transition words used in writing an essay or research paper?
4. How do transition words relate to rhetorical modes of writing in Chapter 2?
5. Discuss the advantages of using a rubric.
6. Describe the differences between a holistic and analytic rubric.
7. Identify and describe the steps in writing an essay or research paper.

References

Capella University. (2006). *MEAL plan*. Capella Writing Center. Retrieved from https://www.capella.edu/interactive-media/onlineWritingCenter/downloads/handoutMEALPlan2006.pdf

Capella University. (2009). *Transitions and transitional phrases*. Retrieved from https://www.capella.edu/interactive-media/onlinewritingcenter/downloads/handouttransitions2009.pdf

Gezie, A., Khaja, K., Chang, V. N., Adamek, M. E., & Johnsen, M. B. (2012). Rubrics as a tool for learning and assessment: What do baccalaureate students think? *Journal of Teaching in Social Work*, *32*(4), 421–437. Retrieved from https://doi.org/10.1080/08841233.2012.705240

Kellogg, R. T. (1988). Attentional overload and writing performance: Effects of rough draft and outline strategies. *Journal of Experimental Psychology: Learning, Memory, and Cognition*, *14*(2), 355–365. Retrieved from http://dx.doi.org.contentproxy.phoenix.edu/10.1037/0278-7393.14.2.355

Manzanares, M. C. S., Baez, M. Á. S., Ortega-Lopez, V., & Manso Villalain, J. M. (2015). Self-regulation and rubrics assessment in structural engineering subjects. *Education Research International; New York*. Retrieved from http://dx.doi.org. /10.1155/2015/340521

Solikhah, I., Pandawa, J. I., & Pucangan, K. (2017). Drafting and revising strategies to develop English essay By EFL Indonesian learners. *IJOLTL: Indonesian Journal of Language Teaching and Linguistics*, *5*(13), 919–930. Retrieved from https://doi.org/10.21474/IJAR01/3591

University of New Brunswick. (n.d.). *Grading rubrics: Set expectations, make feedback delivery more efficient*. Retrieved from http://www.unb.ca/fredericton/cetl/_resources/tls_files/pdfs/teaching_tips/gradingrubrics.pdf

GLOSSARY

Academic assets	The tools and resources available to a student to assist in the writing process.
Academic blogs	Also known as weblogs, blogs contain scholarly, peer-reviewed articles and journals.
Academic integrity	Moral and ethical code that states cheating will be avoided.
Accuracy	Reliability and validity of information.
Affinity diagram	Assists the writer in categorizing and identifying relationships between ideas.
Aggregators	Online reference systems that license content from a wide variety of academic journals, books, periodicals, and primary sources.
American Psychological Association (APA)	Writing and style guidelines used in studies of the behavioral and social sciences.
Analytic rubric	A quantitative element that assigns a score to each section of the rubric. Used for more precise feedback.
Anchor	An anchor link is a web link that allows users to jump to a specific point on a website page.
Annotated bibliography	Gives written information about the content of each reference. The summary serves as the citation information, not the citation itself.
Annotated outline	Adds citation information and provides evidentiary support for each section and topic of an outline.
Annotation	Assists the reader and writer in understanding the text by providing notes, comments, or other information about an article or book.
Argument mapping	A way of laying out visual reasoning and evidence for and against a statement or claim.
Author's responsibility	Accuracy and integrity of a written paper, including formatting according to writing and style guidelines.
Bibliographic manager	A software tool used to store bibliographic information from journals, books, articles, and more.
Bibliographic trail	A retrospective review at the bibliography or reference page of a journal article or book. Used to locate and follow research.

Bibliography	A list of books, magazines, scholarly works, or websites that serves as evidence to support research topic. Also known as references or sources.
Bing query language	Also called Bing Advanced Operator Syntax. A search language that allows the user to refine search queries for more accurate searching.
Blog	Online diary or journal on a website, also called weblog.
Boolean searching	Also called Boolean logic or Boolean operators. Consists of the conjunction words AND, OR, and NOT used in Internet and database searching.
Brainstorming	An idea-generation activity that allows students to generate topic ideas based on facts, impressions, emotions, and reactions.
Cause-and-effect diagram	Also known as the Ishikawa or fishbone diagram. Allows people to organize thoughts about problems and what may be causing them.
Chain of events	Tool that assists in writing a story according to the sequence of events.
Checklist	Written tasks that must be performed.
Chicago Manual of Style	Writing and style guidelines widely used in the publishing industry.
Citation indexing	The researcher views which later documents were cited in earlier documents.
Citation manager	Also called a bibliographic manager or reference manager. Used to store bibliographic information.
Citations	Also known as references or sources, linked to published works such as books, journal articles, or magazines.
Cloud synchronization	File-backup system. Saves files from a desktop or laptop onto another company's server rather than a personal computer.
Content editing	Editing a body of work to ensure your words are correctly communicated to an audience. Content editing is concerned with factual accuracy and inconsistent statements within a paper.
Contingency plan	A backup plan created for emergencies.
Convergence	Allows an author to share research through blog posting, extend its shelf life, and make it accessible to nonspecialists.
Convergent thinking	The grouping, evaluation, and acceptance of ideas for use in a project.
Copyright	Owner-exclusive right to creative works such as books, journal articles, music, and more.
Copyright infringement	Occurs when a copyrighted work is reproduced, distributed, performed, publicly displayed, or made into a derivative (preexisting) work without the permission of the copyright owner.
CRAAAP	Currency, Relevance, Authority, Accuracy, Accessibility, and Purpose.
Database	A repository of information that contains journal articles, newspapers, conference papers, magazines, and much more.
Default	Options that are preselected by a computer software application.
Descriptive annotated bibliography	Seeks to describe the actual reference or source.
Developmental editing	Reorganizes and restructures a body of work; reviews the overall structure of the paper.

Directory of Open-Access Journal	Consists of free, peer-reviewed, no-embargo articles that are immediately available online as soon they are published.
Discovery searching	A unified index source for searching. Only searches one large database, not multiple, to increase the speed of searching.
Divergent thinking	The creative thinking process; the generating and presenting of ideas.
EBSCO	Elton B. Stephens Company is a leading aggregator; EBSCOhost provides full-text access to thousands of periodicals and peer-reviewed journals.
EndNote	A popular fee-based reference-management software used to store bibliographic information.
Evaluative annotated bibliography	Includes both descriptive and summative annotations with the addition of a crucial assessment of the article or book.
Evidentiary support	Scholarly articles to support claims made in the paper. They are fulfilled by using in-text citations.
Ex Libris	Academic database owned by ProQuest.
Exegesis	A critical understanding, interpretation, and explanation of a text. Comes from the Greek *exegeisthai*, "to explain."
Federated searching	Allows the user to retrieve information from multiple sources, namely databases from a single-entry point.
File format	Encoded information that is stored for a particular software application.
Fishbone	See **Cause-and-effect diagram**.
Flexible inclusion	Using different search syntaxes to expand search results.
Flowcharting	Visually listing procedures step by step to solve a problem.
Font	Typeface.
Force-field analysis	A tool that allows the writer to list items for or against a particular topic.
Formal outline	A structured, detailed outline with main points (topics) and supporting points (subtopics) that have parallel structure.
Formatting	Refers to the layout of the paper.
Freewriting	Allows for word association by hopping from one idea to another.
Gale	Another aggregator that houses scholarly literature.
Google Scholar	Free multidisciplinary academic discovery tool that enables the user to search for scholarly literature. Provides a one-stop search location for academic scholarly resources.
Google Special Syntax	Search operators that assist in more precise searching.
Heading	The title at the beginning of a page, new paragraph, or book chapter.
Heading levels	Formatting arrangements of headings.
Holistic rubric	Reviews the quality, proficiency, and understanding of the overall work of the student. Used to give summary feedback.
Hyperlink	A link to another file or document location.
Indentation	One tab or five spaces in the word processor. A signal that a new paragraph is beginning.
Informal outline	Also known as a scratch outline because you are more likely to freewrite. Uses a simple list of main points by using keywords and phrases.

Intellectual property	Creative works such as books, movies, and articles that are owned by a person, group, or organization.
Intentional plagiarism	Direct plagiarism is blatant cheating.
Internet browser	Software program that allows access to the Internet to view web content on the computer.
Ishikawa diagram	See **Cause-and-effect diagram**.
Keyword	A word that is of importance to a concept, document, or Internet search.
Knowledge assets	See **Academic assets**.
Logical and orderly thinking	Writers determine the best method to develop and support arguments. See **Rhetorical modes**.
Main idea	The most important point about a paragraph.
Margins	The separation or space between the edge of the page and the paper's primary content.
MEAL plan	Elements of a paragraph: Main idea, Evidence, Analysis, and Linking.
Mechanical editing	Reviews spelling, grammar, punctuation, capitalization, abbreviations, and formatting of lists, headings, and tables.
Memory recall	The brain's ability to retrieve short- and long-term information.
Mendeley	Free reference-management software used to store bibliographic information.
Metadata	Bibliographic information about books, journals, articles, magazines, or pictures. It is data about the bibliographic data.
Microsoft Academic	Microsoft Academic is a scholarly search engine that uses keyword search to find scholarly literature.
Microsoft Word	Word-processing software application.
Mind maps	Visual representations of thoughts that create associations of ideas, which are connected by words, images, and how people think about a topic.
Mini managers	Small reference managers inside software programs and databases.
Mobile hotspot	Travel routers that allow Internet access from a smartphone.
Modern Language Association (MLA)	*Modern Language Association* writing and style guidelines, often found in the schools of humanities and liberal arts.
Modified annotated outline/bibliography	Combines the outline, annotated outline, and annotated bibliography so the student views how the entire paper is assembled.
Nesting	Term for allowing for an Internet search to be performed in word order. Uses parentheses to include synonyms or alternate terms that may describe your topic.
Online Computer Library Center (OCLC)	The Online Computer Library Center is a global library cooperative where libraries worldwide are members.
Open source	A website that provides free scholarly information to users.
Outline	The strategic portion of writing. Strategy sets direction, focuses effort, provides consistency, and defines organization within a paper.
Page numbers	Number assigned to a document such as an essay or research paper. Locators to help find information in a book, journal, or article.

Paragraph	A group of sentences that support a main idea. Usually between four to six sentences long.
Paraphrasing	Converts the material from one source into the writer's own words.
Patent	Sole rights to an invention that was approved by the government for a limited period of time.
Phrase searching	Involves using quotation marks around two or more keywords.
Plagiarism	Intellectual theft of text, data, PowerPoints, spreadsheets, knowledge, or ideas.
Portals	Customized and integrated doorways to various information resources, services, and websites through a single access point.
PowerPoint	A slideshow-presentation software program used to present material from essays, research papers, books, and articles.
Prewriting	The beginning stage of writing where the writer investigates a topic and writes their thoughts using paper or a computer.
Principles of organization	A form of effective writing that uses rhetorical modes or logical and orderly thinking
Process mapping	See **Flowcharting**.
Proofreading	The final check for errors in a document.
ProQuest	Leading aggregator that houses full-text coverage of thousands of periodicals and peer-reviewed journals.
Pros and cons	List of reasons for or against an issue.
Pros, cons, faults, and fixes	List of reasons for or against an issue, including a proposed solution for each pro and con.
Quoting	Repeating another source word for word using quotation marks.
REAP	Revising, editing, accuracy, and proofreading.
Reference manager	Also called bibliographic manager or citation manager. Used to store bibliographic information.
Reference-management life cycle	Activities performed after the discovery of literature: create, store, organize, cite, change, and share.
References	A list of books, magazines, scholarly work, or websites that serves as evidence to support research topic. Also known as a bibliography or sources.
RefWorks	A fee-based reference manager that can be purchased by individuals.
Research	Locating scholarly articles, journals, magazines, and websites as evidence to support a topic.
Revising	To reexamine, rethink, straighten out, review, and reappraise a paper.
Rhetorical mode	How a writer communicates through language and writing. Which mode the writer chooses depends on his or her purpose for writing.
Rubric	Grading guide that breaks down the instructions of the assignment and places point values on each section required.
Ruler	Used in most word-processing programs; it measures the layout on a page.
Scholarly blog	Also known as academic blogs, they contain scholarly, peer-reviewed articles and journals.

Scope creep	Going outside the boundaries of the writing project.
Self-plagiarism	Using one's own work as new and original.
Seminal work	Landmark original research. Seminal comes from the word semen, which mean seed. Also called germinal work.
Sequence	Events or processes told in a particular order. First, second, third, and fourth is a form of sequence.
Smartphone	Handheld personal computer, telephone, and camera with Internet access.
Sources	A list of books, magazines, scholarly works, or websites. Also known as bibliography or references.
Storyboarding	A tool that assists the writer in telling a story in segments.
Strategy	A plan, pattern, position, perspective, and ploy created to achieve a goal.
Structured analytic technique	Tools used to organize and structure the thought process to encourage problem-solving.
Student academic assets	See **Academic Assets.**
Summarizing	Taking ideas from a large passage of one source and placing the main points into your own words.
Summative annotated bibliography	Summarizes the content, message, or argument of the annotated bibliography.
SWOTT analysis	Strengths, weaknesses, opportunity, threats, and trends. Helpful in providing a strong argument for making a decision.
Syntax	A formation or group of words allowing formalized search and access to information on the Internet.
Table of contents	A table of contents (TOC) is a comprehensive representation of the headings and subheadings in your document.
Team collaboration	Working together with other people in a joint effort to achieve a common goal.
Template	A guide or preset format for a document.
Temporal citation	Bibliographic information that moves forward or backward in time.
The Chicago Manual of Style (Chicago)	Writing and style guidelines used in the publishing industry.
Thesis statement	A point of view that is arguable, persuasive, or a reminder of a major claim that can be defended with scholarly evidence. The thesis statement is the purpose of the paper, the "why" or "how."
Time management	Using time efficiently and effectively to accomplish a task.
Topic	A subject of discussion.
Trademark	A symbol, word, or design that is registered with the pto.gov as a unique expression of that organization. Logos are an example of designs that can be trademarked.
Transition words	Words that are used to connect ideas.
Unintentional plagiarism	Plagiarism occurs accidently; it is perceived as innocent plagiarism that occurs due to a lack of writing skill and knowledge.
Validity	Information was collected using sound research methods and was correctly cited when published.

Wikipedia	Open-source encyclopedia that is collaboratively edited online.
Wild card	Also called truncation. A search syntax that is supported by the asterisk (*) symbol. Each asterisk represents a word replacement or placeholder for the remainder of the phrase.
Word processor	Software application that is used for writing, printing, and publishing of the written word.
WorldCat	World Catalog. A library catalog where information is discovered globally.
Zotero	Popular free reference-management software touted as a personal research assistant. Used to store bibliographic information.

INDEX

C

Calculator, 82–83
Capital campaign and fundraising theory, 65
Cause and effect, 32–33
Chain of events, 27
Charismatic leadership, 59
Checklists, 129–137
    assignment guidelines, 132
    body, 131
    citations/references, 132
    conclusion, 131
    paragraph development, 131
    sentence development, 131
Chicago Manual of Style (Chicago) guidelines, 1, 3
Citation indexing, 73–74
Citation managers, 119
Clarity in writing, 129
Classification, 29–31
    affinity diagram, 30
    division and, 29–31
Cloud synchronization, 121
Comments, 57
Companion guide, xvii
Compare and contrast, 33–35
Content editing, 132
Contingency plan, 2–3
Contingency planning, xvi
Convergence, 114
Convergent-thinking phase, 20
Copyright infringement, 140
Copyrights, 139
Currency, Relevance, Authority, Accuracy, Accessibility, and Purpose (CRAAAP), 91

D

Databases, 92–93
Date range, 80
Default font, 5
Definition, 31–32, 82
Description, 29
Descriptive annotated bibliography, 61

Developmental editing, 132
Directory of Open-Access Journals (DOAJ), 103–105
    user navigation and searching, 104
Discovery searching, 98–103
    EBSCO Discovery, 102–103
    Ex Libris, 99
    ProQuest summon, 100–102
    WorldCat, 99
Divergent-thinking phase, 20
Division, 29–31
Drafting, xv, 149–154
    instructions, 155–156
    meal, 150
    outline, 149–150
    rubrics, 153–155
        analytic rubric, 154
        holistic rubric, 154
    transition words, 150–153

E

EBSCO Discovery, 102–103
EBSCOhost, 94–95
Editing, xv, 132–136. *See also* Content editing; Developmental editing; Mechanical editing
    time for, 133–134
EndNote, 122
Evaluative annotated bibliography, 62–64
Ex Libris, 99
Exclusion, 77
Exegesis, 57
Exemplification or illustration, 29
Explanations, 57

F

Federated searching, 93–94
File format, 81
Filetype, 81
Final paper, xv
Fishbone diagram, 32
    brainstorming, 33
    development, 33
    prioritizing, 33

KEY TOOLS OF WRITING AND RESEARCH *A Guide for the Student Writer*

U

Unintentional plagiarism, 140
Unit converter, 83–84
Universal Resource Locators (URL), 79

V

Validity, 75

W

Warm-glow giving theory, 65
Web-based plagiarism-software tool, 144
Wikipedia trail, 74–75
Wild cards, 78
Word processor, 3
WorldCat, 99
Writing process, xv, 1–16
    adobe flash player, 15
    adobe reader, 14
    assignment, assessing, 1–2
    author's responsibility, 4
    clarity in, 129

    contingency plan, 2–3
    default font, 5
    formatting, 4
        font, 4–5
        margins, 5
        page number, 9
    grammar checking, 11–13
    headings, 9–11
        levels, 10
    internet browsers, 13–14
    java, 15
    knowledge assets, 2
    knowledge management, 2
    Microsoft office compatibility pack, 15
    Microsoft word readiness, 3–4
    mobile hotspot, 3
    paragraphs and indentation, 7
    proofing, 12
    ruler, 8–9
    spelling checking, 11–13

Z

Zotero, 121